100 UNDER 500 CALORIE VEGETARIAN RECIPES

Low Calorie Vegetarian and Vegan Meals

by
Beth Christian

100 Under 500 Calorie Vegetarian Recipes

Copyright © 2013
MadeGlobal Publishing

ISBN-13: 978-1492325154
ISBN-10: 1492325155

All rights reserved. No part of this publication may be reproduced, stored in a retrieval system, or transmitted, in any form or by any means, electronic, mechanical, photocopying, recording or otherwise, except as permitted by the UK Copyright, Designs and Patents Act 1988, without the prior permission of the publisher.

M
MadeGlobal Publishing

For more information on
MadeGlobal Publishing, visit our website:
www.madeglobal.com

Disclaimer

The recipes provided in this book are designed to aid the reader with a calorie-controlled diet, they are not a diet in themselves. This book is not intended to be a substitute for consulting with your physician and any dietary change should be discussed with your physician, particularly if you have a medical condition. Neither the publisher nor the author shall be liable or responsible for any loss, damage or adverse reaction allegedly arising from the information or recipes given in this book.

Any use of trademarks, specific products, companies or manufacturers in this book does not imply any endorsement or connection with that product or company. Alternative products exist and may be more suitable for use in your case. These are simply suggestions which were used in the making of the recipes.

While the author has made every effort to give accurate measurements, calorie counts, names of publications and website addresses, neither the author nor the publisher assumes any responsibility for errors or changes that occur after publication. The author and publisher also do not take any responsibility for third party books, websites and their content.

Contents

Introduction   1

Starters   5

1. Tuscan Style Hummus 6
2. Sun-Dried Tomato Hummus 7
3. Black Bean and Corn Salsa.................................... 8
4. Chunky Guacamole 9
5. Roasted Pepper and Pesto Cheese Spread.............10
6. Cranberry Goat Cheese Log..................................11
7. Broccoli Cheese Baked Potato Skins 12
8. Quick Microwave Nachos.....................................14
9. Quiche Hors d'Oeuvres 15
10. Greek Eggplant Rounds 16

Soups   19

11. Vegetarian Split Pea Soup.................................... 20
12. Vegetable Tortilla Gumbo.................................... 22
13. Italian Garlic and Pasta Soup 24
14. Creamy Chilled Zucchini and Watercress Soup .. 26
15. Creamy Broccoli and Cheddar Soup.................... 28
16. Cream of Celery Soup.. 30
17. Pumpkin Butternut Bisque 32

18.	Butter Bean and Kale Soup	34
19.	Hearty Italian Bean Soup	36
20.	Portobello Mushroom Barley Soup	38

Meatless Makeovers   *41*

21.	Moussaka	42
22.	Vegan Baked Rigatoni with Tofu	44
23.	Vegetable Garden Goulash	46
24.	Oven Baked Vegetarian Paella	48
25.	Vegetarian "Veal" Parmesan	50
26.	Spicy Sausage and Peppers	52
27.	Where's the "Beef" Stroganoff	54
28.	Vegan Stuffed Peppers	56

Pasta and Noodles   *59*

29.	Pasta and Fagioli	60
30.	Penne with Sun-Dried Tomato Pesto	62
31.	Spinach Spaghetti Puttanesca	64
32.	Harvest Whole Wheat Lasagne	66
33.	Linguine with Broccoli Rabe and Tempeh	68
34.	Best Ever Baked Ziti	70
35.	Mushroom Tortellini with Walnuts	72
36.	Pumpkin Ravioli with Pepitas	74
37.	Gnocchi with Garlic Sautéed Broccoli	76
38.	Farfalle and Kasha with Sweet Onions and Carrots	78

39.	Vegan Stuffed Shells	80
40.	Vegan Spaghetti "Bolognese"	82
41.	Plum-Glazed Tofu and Rice Noodles	84
42.	Pad Thai Noodle Wraps	86
43.	Divine Noodle Kugel	88

Pizzas and Sandwiches 91

44.	Week Night Thin Crust Pizza	92
45.	Autumn Delight Pizza	94
46.	Broccoli and Ricotta Pizza	95
47.	Greek Salad Pita Pizza	96
48.	Grilled Vegetable Pizza	98
49.	Whole Grain Open Face Veggie Club	99
50.	Bean and Artichoke Panini	100
51.	Curry Tofu Salad Pita Pockets	101
52.	Hummus and Greek Salad Wrap	102
53.	Grilled Eggplant and Mozzarella Burger	103

Rice, Grains and Beans 105

54.	Cajun Red Beans and Rice	106
55.	Lentil and Couscous Curry	108
56.	Ratatouille Quinoa Casserole	110
57.	Risotto with Cabbage and Chickpeas	112
58.	Mushroom Medley Barley Risotto	114
59.	Brown Rice and Butternut Risotto	116

60.	Southern Smokehouse Hoppin' John	118
61.	DIY Refried Beans and Rice	120
62.	Cornmeal Chili Bean Casserole	122
63.	Middle Eastern Falafel Patties	124
64.	Brown Rice Tabbouleh	126
65.	Quinoa with Cashews	128

Ways with Eggs   131

66.	French Herb Omelet	132
67.	Going Greek Frittata	134
68.	Tofu and Egg Burrito Wrap	136
69.	Quick Microwave Egg and Cheese Sandwich	137
70.	Home on the Range Huevos Rancheros	138
71.	Vegetarian Eggs Benedict	140
72.	Super Southwest Omelet	142
73.	Baked Asparagus Frittata	144
74.	Spinach and Mushroom Frittata	146
75.	Italian Eggs in Purgatory	148

Salads   151

76.	Lightened Up Coleslaw	152
77.	Spinach Salad with Blackberries and Goat Cheese	153
78.	Baby Potato Salad with Mint and Peas	154
79.	Pasta Primavera Salad	155
80.	Sesame Peanut Noodle Salad	156

81.	Turkish Bulgur Wheat Salad	157
82.	Orange Wheat Berry Salad	158
83.	Crispy Sweet and Sour Slaw	160
84.	Carrot, Walnut 'n Raisin Salad	161
85.	Picnic Macaroni Salad	162
86.	Easy Pinto Bean Taco Salad	164
87.	New Style Waldorf Salad	166
88.	Nutty Cranberry Broccoli Salad	168
89.	German Style Potato Salad	170
90.	Thai Cucumber Salad	172

Vegan desserts   *173*

91.	Apple Cinnamon Compote	174
92.	Summer Peach Sorbet	175
93.	Banana Basmati Rice Pudding	176
94.	Avocado Sorbet	178
95.	Grilled Mango with Coconut Cream	179
96.	Strawberry Phyllo Pocket	180
97.	Simple Watermelon Slushy	182
98.	Choco-Coconut Ice Cream	183
99.	Vegan Vanilla Soy Pudding	184
100.	Vegan Pumpkin Pie Pudding	185

Glossary and Substitutions 187

*Temperature and Weight
Conversion Charts* 193

Introduction

When 100 Under 500 Calorie Meals was published, a few of my friends commented on how they would have liked more calorie-counted vegetarian and vegan recipes, so I've worked closely with chef and nutritionist Liz Scott to devise the recipes found in this book. We've chosen recipes that can be mixed and matched – starters plus mains/entrées or mains/entrées plus desserts – to produce a meal that comes to no more than 500 calories. This recipe book was devised to go with my book **Easy Alternate Day Fasting: Fast and Feast Your Way to a New You,** but it is suitable for use with any low-calorie diet or by people who just want to cut down and eat more healthily.

Each recipe states how many servings there are, and the calorie count per serving. It is easy to keep track of the calorie-count and also adapt the recipe to serve different numbers of people. If you're like me, you don't want to scrimp on taste when you're following a healthy eating plan, so these recipes are tasty, nutritious and low-calorie – you really don't have to compromise.

I've also made every effort to highlight simple changes that can be made to ensure the recipes are suitable for vegans too. That way I hope everyone can enjoy these meals as much as I do!

If you're interested in learning more about Alternate Day Fasting, which actually isn't fasting at all, then check out the website http://www.EasyAlternateDayFasting.com and my book **Easy Alternate Day Fasting: Fast and Feast Your Way to a New You.** It's the only healthy eating plan that I have ever stuck to and it's all because you don't have to count calories and be good all of the time – perfect.

Beth Christian

STARTERS

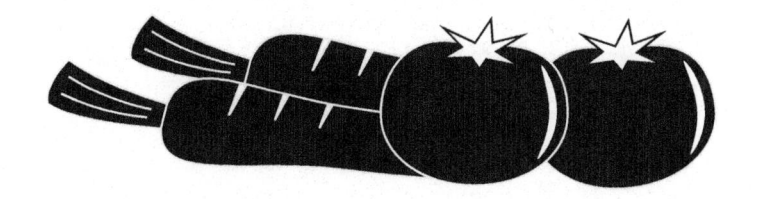

1... Tuscan Style Hummus

Here the usual chickpeas are replaced by cannellini beans and flavored with aromatic rosemary for a delicious start to an Italian meal.

Ingredients

- 1 can (15-ounce) cannellini beans, drained and rinsed
- 1 garlic clove, roughly chopped
- 1 tbsp. lemon juice
- ½ tsp. dried rosemary
- 2 tsp. extra virgin olive oil plus more for drizzling
- Salt and pepper to taste
- Raw vegetables for dipping such as celery, fennel, carrots, or bell peppers

Directions

1. Puree all the ingredients in a food processor until smooth. Transfer to a bowl, cover and keep chilled until ready to serve with the vegetables.

Information

Makes 4 servings
Each serving has 150 calories

2...Sun-Dried Tomato Hummus

The flavorful addition of sun-dried tomatoes adds great flavor in this popular Middle Eastern dip made with tahini.

Ingredients

- 1 can (15-ounce) chickpeas, drained and rinsed
- 2 garlic cloves, roughly chopped
- ¼ cup marinated sun-dried tomatoes, drained and roughly chopped
- 1 tbsp. cup tahini
- 1 tbsp. lemon juice
- Salt and pepper to taste
- Raw vegetables or low-fat pita chips to serve

Directions

1. Puree all ingredients in a food processor until smooth. Transfer to a bowl, cover, and keep chilled until ready to serve.

Information

Makes 4 servings
Each serving has 170 calories

3... Black Bean and Corn Salsa

The perfect start to a Mexican meal, this fiber-rich dip can be made as spicy or mild as you wish.

Ingredients

- 1 can (15-ounce) black beans, drained and rinsed
- 1 can (3-ounce) corn kernels, drained
- ½ medium red bell pepper, seeded and diced
- 1 medium jalapeno pepper, seeded and diced (optional or more to taste)
- 3 green onions, chopped
- 1 tbsp. lime juice
- 1 tsp. red wine vinegar
- 1 tbsp. olive oil
- ½ tsp. ground cumin
- 1 Tb chopped fresh cilantro
- Salt and pepper to taste
- Baked corn tortilla chips for dipping

Directions

1. In a medium bowl combine black beans, corn, bell pepper, jalapeno pepper and green onions.
2. In a small bowl whisk together lime juice, vinegar, olive oil and cumin. Add to bean mixture, stiring to coat.
3. Stir in cilantro, season with salt and pepper and serve with tortilla chips. Keep refrigerated up to 1 week.

Information

Makes 6 servings
Each serving has 135 calories

4... Chunky Guacamole

Here's an easy version of everyone's favorite dip that also replaces the usual sour cream with Greek yogurt for a leaner but no less flavorful rendition.

Ingredients

- 2 small ripe Hass avocados
- ½ tbsp. lime juice
- 2 heaping tbsp. fat free prepared salsa, mild or hot
- 1 tbsp. nonfat plain Greek yogurt
- Bell pepper scoops and baked corn or multigrain tortilla chips for dipping

Directions

1. Cut each avocado in half lengthwise and twist apart. Discard seed and scoop out flesh into a medium bowl. Add lime juice and mash, using the back of a fork, until smooth yet slightly chunky.

2. Stir in salsa and yogurt, transfer to a clean bowl and serve immediately. To store, cover surface with plastic wrap and refrigerate up to 1 day.

Information

Makes 4 servings
Each serving has 165 calories
For Vegan: substitute soy yogurt for the Greek yogurt

5... Roasted Pepper and Pesto Cheese Spread

Enjoy this flavorful spread as an hors d'oeuvre before pasta or other Italian inspired dish, made diet-friendly with nonfat cream cheese.

Ingredients

- 1 tub (8-ounce) nonfat cream cheese, softened
- 2 tbsp. prepared pesto sauce
- 2 tbsp. minced roasted red bell pepper
- Fresh ground pepper to taste
- Melba toast or baked crackers for serving

Directions

1. In a medium bowl beat together cream cheese, pesto, bell pepper and ground pepper. Transfer to a serving bowl, cover and chill for at least 1 hour to allow flavors to combine.
2. Keep leftovers covered in the refrigerator for up to 1 week.

Information

Makes 6 servings
Each serving has 130 calories
For Vegan: substitute soy cream cheese such as Tofutti for dairy cream cheese

6... Cranberry Goat Cheese Log

The creamy richness of goat cheese, surprisingly low in fat and calories, is complimented by a sweet and satisfying coating in this show stopper of spreads.

Ingredients

- ½ cup reduced-sugar dried cranberries, chopped
- ¼ tsp. ground cinnamon
- 1 log (11-ounce) goat cheese
- 1 tbsp. honey or agave nectar
- Reduced fat stoned wheat crackers for serving

Directions

- In a small bowl stir together cranberries and cinnamon. Spread out on a 12-inch long piece of parchment paper.
- Place whole goat cheese log on to mixture and gently press and roll until completely covered.
- Transfer to a platter, drizzle honey over, and serve with crackers. Keep refrigerated in an airtight container for up to 10 days.

Information

Makes 8 servings
Each serving has 172 calories

7...Broccoli Cheese Baked Potato Skins

Who knew this favorite appetizer could be diet friendly with just a little tweaking. Enjoy with a dollop of plain Greek or soy yogurt instead of the usual sour cream.

Ingredients

- 2 small Idaho or russet potatoes
- Light olive oil cooking spray
- Salt and pepper to taste
- 1 cup small broccoli florets, cooked to crisp tender
- ¼ cup reduced fat shredded cheddar cheese

Directions

1. Preheat the oven to 375 °F. Bake potatoes until fork tender, about 35 minutes.

2. When potatoes are cool enough to handle, cut each lengthwise into halves, and scoop out all but ¼ inch of potato next to skin. Spray with the oil, season with salt and pepper, and place cut side down on a baking sheet.

3. Increase oven temperature to 425 °F and bake potato halves until golden and crispy, about 12 minutes.

4. Turn potatoes cut side up; fill each with broccoli, sprinkle cheese over and return to oven until cheese is melted, about 5 minutes.

5. Serve immediately.

Information

Makes 2 servings
Each serving has 180 calories
For Vegan: substitute dairy-free cheddar for regular cheddar

8...Quick Microwave Nachos

Easy to make but hard to resist, healthy and protein-rich pinto beans highlight this ever-popular Tex-Mex treat.

Ingredients

- 12 baked corn tortilla chips
- ½ cup canned pinto beans, drained and rinsed
- 1/3 cup reduced fat shredded cheddar or Monterey Jack cheese
- 2 tbsp. canned jalapeno slices
- 2 tbsp. sliced black olives
- 1 small plum tomato, diced
- 2 green onions, chopped
- Dollop of plain nonfat Greek or soy yogurt

Directions

1. Arrange tortilla chips on a microwave-safe plate, overlapping as necessary. Distribute beans over chips and top with cheese and jalapeno slices.

2. Microwave on high until cheese is melted and beans are heated through, 1 to 2 minutes.

3. Sprinkle with olives, tomato, and green onions, and serve immediately with yogurt on top.

Information

Makes 2 servings

Starters

Each serving has 190 calories

9... Quiche Hors d'Oeuvres

Bake these ahead and have ready for a quick and delicious appetizer while waiting for dinner to be served

Ingredients

- 1 (9 oz) pkg. frozen chopped spinach
- ¾ cup shredded reduced-fat cheddar cheese
- 2 large eggs, beaten
- 3 large egg whites, beaten
- ¼ medium red bell pepper, diced
- ¼ medium onion, finely diced
- Salt and pepper to taste

Directions

1. Preheat the oven to 350 °F. Lightly coat a 12 cup muffin tin with cooking spray.

2. Cook the spinach according to package directions and squeeze dry of excess liquid. In a medium bowl combine the spinach with the remaining ingredients and stir well.

3. Divide between the muffin cups and bake for 20 minutes, or until a tester comes out clean.

Information

Makes 6 servings
Each serving has 125 calories

10... Greek Eggplant Rounds

This healthy starter is perfect before any Mediterranean inspired meal including pasta or pairs well with a simple salad as well for a light lunch.

Ingredients

- 1 medium eggplant, unpeeled
- Light olive oil cooking spray
- Salt and pepper to taste
- ½ cup reduced fat crumbled feta cheese
- 2 tsp. dried oregano
- ½ cup prepared roasted red peppers, chopped
- ¼ cup pitted Kalamata olives, roughly chopped
- 4 fresh basil sprigs

Directions

1. Preheat oven to 350 °F. Trim ends of eggplant and slice into 8 ½-inch rounds.

2. Place eggplant on a large baking sheet; lightly spray both sides of slices with olive oil and season with salt and pepper. Bake, turning over once, until softened and lightly browned, about 20 minutes.

3. Top each round with feta cheese, oregano, roasted red peppers and olives. Return to oven and bake until cheese begins to melt, about 5 minutes. Transfer to a platter or individual plates and garnish each round with the chopped fresh basil. Serve immediately.

Information

Makes 4 servings
Each serving has 110 calories
For Vegan: substitute your choice of nondairy crumbled cheese for the feta

Soups

11... Vegetarian Split Pea Soup

Thick, rich, and flavorful, this low fat version will stick to your ribs and satisfy your appetite for a bowl of hearty goodness. Serve with a large tossed salad and wholegrain roll for a complete dinner.

Ingredients

- 1 tbsp. olive oil
- 1 medium onion, diced
- 1 medium celery stalk, diced
- 1 medium carrot, diced
- 6 cups low-sodium vegetable broth or water
- 1 pkg. (16 oz.) dried green split peas, picked over and rinsed
- Salt and pepper to taste

Directions

1. Heat the oil in a soup pot over medium heat, add onion, celery and carrots, and cook until softened, 8 to 10 minutes, stirring often.

2. Stir in broth and split peas, increase heat to high, and bring to a boil. Reduce heat to medium-low and cook at a simmer, stirring occasionally, until peas are tender, 35 to 40 minutes. Add a touch of water to thin if necessary.

3. Season with salt and pepper and serve.

Soups

INFORMATION

Makes 6 servings
Each serving has 220 calories

12... Vegetable Tortilla Gumbo

Flavor, fiber, and protein from beans are featured in this satisfying soup with the kick of hot spices for extra fat burning.

Ingredients

- 2 tbsp. canola oil
- 2 tbsp. all-purpose flour
- 1 medium onion, diced
- 1 medium celery stalk, diced
- 1 medium green bell pepper, seeded and diced
- 1 garlic clove, minced
- 1 ½ cups frozen cut okra
- 1 cup frozen corn and lima beans (succotash)
- 1 can (15 oz.) stewed tomatoes, chopped
- 6 cups low-sodium vegetable broth or water
- 1 tbsp. chili powder
- ¼ tsp. cayenne pepper, or more to taste
- 1 cup canned black beans, drained and rinsed
- ¾ cup coarsely broken baked corn tortilla chips

Directions

1. Whisk together oil and flour blend over medium-high heat in a soup pot until dark and smooth, about 5 minutes.

Soups

2. Stir in onion, celery, and green bell pepper and cook, stirring often, until softened, 4 to 6 minutes. Add garlic, okra, succotash, and tomatoes, stir well to combine, and cook a further minute.

3. Add broth, chili powder and cayenne pepper, increase heat to high and bring to a boil. Reduce heat to medium-low and cook at a simmer, stirring occasionally, for 20 minutes.

4. Add black beans, and half the tortilla chips, and cook 10 minutes more. Ladle into soup bowls and top with remaining chips before serving.

INFORMATION

Makes 6 servings
Each serving has 248 calories

13...Italian Garlic and Pasta Soup

The bold flavor of garlic highlights this soothing soup, made fiber rich with whole wheat pasta and vegetables. Perfect as a side for tossed greens or an Italian-style bean salad.

Ingredients

- 1 tbsp. olive oil
- 1 small onion, diced
- 2 medium carrots, diced
- 1 medium celery stalk, diced
- 6 garlic cloves, minced
- 2 cups spinach leaves, stems removed
- 3 cups low-sodium vegetable broth or water
- 2 cups water
- 1 bay leaf
- 2 cups cooked whole wheat pasta such as shells or ditalini
- Salt and pepper to taste
- Grated parmesan cheese for serving (optional)

Directions

1. Heat olive oil in a soup pot over medium heat, add onion, carrot, and celery, and cook until slightly softened, about 3 minutes, stirring often.

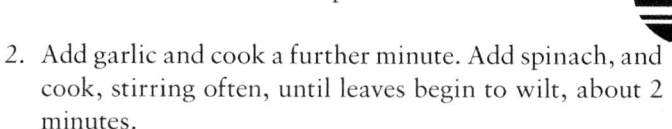

2. Add garlic and cook a further minute. Add spinach, and cook, stirring often, until leaves begin to wilt, about 2 minutes.

3. Pour in broth and water, add bay leaf, increase heat to high and bring to a boil. Reduce heat to medium-low and cook at a simmer, stirring occasionally, until vegetables are tender, about 12 minutes.

4. Stir in the cooked pasta, bring back to a simmer and cook for 3 minutes until piping hot. Season with salt and pepper and serve immediately with a sprinkling of parmesan cheese on top if desired.

INFORMATION

Makes 4 servings
Each serving has 180 calories

14... CREAMY CHILLED ZUCCHINI AND WATERCRESS SOUP

Refreshing and satisfying, this perfect summer soup is great to serve before a pasta or rice salad or entrée.

INGREDIENTS

- 1 tbsp. olive oil
- 1 medium onion, chopped
- 1 large garlic clove, minced
- 1 lb zucchini, trimmed and roughly chopped
- Salt and pepper to taste
- 3 cups low-sodium vegetable broth or water
- 1 sprig thyme
- 2 cups packed watercress, tough stems removed
- ½ cup plain low-fat Greek yogurt
- 1 tbsp. finely chopped chives or fresh herbs of choice

DIRECTIONS

1. In a saucepan heat the oil over medium-high heat. Add the onions and cook, stirring often, for 3 minutes. Add the garlic and cook 1 minute more. Add the zucchini, salt and pepper, and stir well to coat. Add the broth and thyme and bring to a boil. Reduce the heat and simmer, stirring occasionally, for 20 minutes.

2. Stir in the watercress and continue to cook for 5 minutes. Remove from the heat and discard the thyme sprig. With a hand-held immersion blender or in batches in a food processor, puree the soup until smooth. Transfer to a clean saucepan and whisk in the yogurt. Do not reheat. Taste for seasoning, allow to cool somewhat, then refrigerate until well chilled, about 1 hour.

3. To serve, ladle into soup bowls or mugs and top with the chopped chives.

INFORMATION

Makes 4 servings
Each serving has 100 calories
For Vegan: substitute soy yogurt or dairy-free sour cream for the Greek yogurt

15...Creamy Broccoli and Cheddar Soup

Lightened up but no less satisfying, this soup is a great lunch or dinner selection with a salad on the side and a few nonfat croutons on top.

Ingredients

- 1 ½ lb. broccoli, cut into florets and pieces
- 1 medium onion, roughly chopped
- 1 large Idaho or russet potato, peeled and diced
- 4 cups low-sodium vegetable broth or water
- 1 tsp. lemon juice
- ½ cup fat free half and half
- 2/3 cup reduced fat shredded cheddar cheese
- Salt and pepper to taste

Directions

1. In a large soup pot combine the broccoli, onion, potato, broth, and lemon juice. Bring mixture to a boil, reduce the heat to low, and simmer until the vegetables are tender, about 25 minutes.

2. Remove from the heat and begin ladling into a blender. Working in batches, blend until smooth and transfer to a clean saucepan. You can also use a hand held immersion blender the puree the soup directly in the pot.

3. Stir in the half and half and cheese, taste for the addition of salt and pepper and serve hot.

Information

Makes 4 servings
Each serving has 205 calories
For Vegan: substitute soy creamer or milk for the half and half and vegan cheddar-style cheese for the regular cheddar

16… Cream of Celery Soup

Uniquely aromatic celery root combines with regular stalk celery to create a satisfying creamed soup that's full of flavor and delicious served hot or cold.

Ingredients

- 1 tbsp. olive oil
- 1 medium onion, diced
- ½ bunch celery, trimmed and chopped
- 2 medium celeriac (celery root) peeled, and chopped
- Salt and pepper to taste
- 4 cups low-sodium vegetable broth or water
- ½ cup fat free half and half
- 1 tbsp. finely chopped parsley leaves

Directions

1. Heat the oil in a large soup pot over medium heat. Add the onion and cook, stirring often, until soft but not browned, about 4 minutes.

2. Stir in the chopped celery and celeriac, season with salt and pepper, and continue to cook, stirring often, for 2 minutes.

3. Pour in the broth, bring to a boil, reduce the heat to low, and simmer until the vegetables are fork tender, about 15 minutes.

4. Remove from the heat and begin ladling into a blender. Working in batches, blend until smooth and transfer to a clean saucepan. Stir in the half and half.

5. Reheat the blended soup over low heat and season to taste with salt and pepper. Serve topped with the parsley, or chill in the refrigerator and serve cold.

Information

Makes 6 servings
Each serving has 140 calories
For Vegan: substitute soy creamer or milk for the half and half

17...Pumpkin Butternut Bisque

Slightly sweet, silky smooth, and fragrant with the autumn spices of ginger, cinnamon, and nutmeg this soup will hit the spot any time of year.

Ingredients

- 1 tbsp. olive oil
- 1 medium leek, white part only, sliced
- Salt and pepper to taste
- 1 medium butternut squash, peeled, seeded and diced
- 1 can (15 oz.) unsweetened pumpkin puree
- 4 cups low-sodium vegetable broth or water
- 1 tbsp. light brown sugar, firmly packed
- ½ tsp. ground ginger
- ½ tsp. ground cinnamon
- Dash ground nutmeg
- 1 cup almond milk
- Sliced almonds for garnish

Directions

1. Heat the oil in a large soup pot over medium heat. Add the leek, season with salt and pepper, and cook, stirring often, until soft but not browned, about 4 minutes.

2. Add the butternut squash and stir to coat.

3. Add the pumpkin puree, broth, brown sugar, ginger, cinnamon, and nutmeg, and stir well to combine. Bring to a boil, reduce the heat to low, and simmer until the squash is fork tender, 12 to 15 minutes.

4. Stir in the almond milk and cook a further minute.

5. Remove from the heat and begin ladling into a blender. Working in batches, blend until smooth and transfer to a clean saucepan.

6. Taste for seasoning and serve hot topped with the sliced almonds.

Information

Makes 6 servings
Each serving has 145 calories

18...Butter Bean and Kale Soup

Rich, creamy butter beans combine with calcium-rich kale in this hearty soup that's accented with sweet bits of carrot pieces and lots of bold and fragrant garlic.

Ingredients

- 1 tbsp. olive oil
- 1 small onion, diced
- 1 medium carrot, diced
- Salt and pepper to taste
- 4 large garlic cloves, minced
- 4 cups roughly chopped kale leaves, stems removed
- 4 cups low-sodium vegetable broth or water
- 1 tsp. dried rubbed sage
- 2 cans (15 oz.) butter beans, drained and rinsed

Directions

1. Heat the olive oil in a large soup pot over medium heat. Add the onion and carrot, season with salt and pepper, and cook, stirring often, until soft but not browned, about 3 minutes.

2. Stir in the garlic and cook a further minute. Add the kale and stir to coat.

3. Pour in the broth and add the sage, stir to combine, and bring to a boil. Reduce the heat to low and simmer until the kale is tender, about 18 minutes.

4. Add the beans and cook for 3 to 5 minutes until heated through.

5. Remove from the heat and using a hand held immersion blender, briefly blend just to thicken slightly but leaving most of the beans whole.

6. Taste for seasoning and serve piping hot.

INFORMATION

Makes 6 servings
Each serving has 138 calories

19...Hearty Italian Bean Soup

This hearty three bean soup with hints of aromatic thyme and the bold taste of garlic is great with a wholegrain roll for dipping and a large Italian-style tossed salad as an accompaniment.

Ingredients

- 1 tbsp. olive oil
- 1 medium onion, diced
- 2 large garlic cloves, minced
- 4 cups low-sodium vegetable broth or water
- 1 (8 oz) can low-sodium tomato sauce
- 1 tsp. dried thyme
- 1 can (15 oz.) Roman beans or red kidney beans
- 1 can (15 oz.) cannellini beans
- 1 can (15 oz.) small pink beans
- 1 tbsp. balsamic vinegar
- Salt and pepper to taste

Directions

1. Heat the olive oil in a large soup pot over medium heat. Add the onion, season with salt and pepper, and cook until the onions are soft, stirring occasionally, about 4 minutes. Add the garlic and cook a further 2 minutes.

2. Pour in the broth and tomato sauce, add the thyme and bring to a boil, stirring occasionally. Add the Roman beans, cannellini beans, and pink beans, stir well and cook at a low simmer for 10 minutes.

3. Remove from the heat, and using a hand held immersion blender or a potato masher, break down the beans until the mixture is thick but still chunky.

4. Return to a low heat and while soup is simmering, stir in the balsamic vinegar. Taste for the addition of salt and pepper, and serve immediately.

INFORMATION

Makes 6 servings
Each serving has 279 calories

20...Portobello Mushroom Barley Soup

Nutritious barley combines with earthy Portobello mushrooms for a soup that's practically a meal in itself.

Ingredients

- 1 tbsp. olive oil
- 1 medium onion, diced
- 1 medium celery stalk, diced
- Salt and pepper to taste
- 2 Portobello mushrooms, stems and gills removed, caps roughly chopped
- 2 garlic cloves, minced
- 4 cups low-sodium vegetable broth or water
- 2/3 cup pearl barley
- 1 tbsp. chopped fresh dill
- 2 tsp. chopped fresh parsley

Directions:

1. Heat the olive oil in a soup pot over medium heat. Add the onion and celery to the pot, season with salt and pepper and cook, stirring often until soft, about 5 minutes. Add the mushrooms and garlic, sprinkle with salt, and continue to cook for 3 minutes, stirring occasionally.

2. Pour in the broth and bring to a boil. Reduce the heat to low and cook for 5 minutes.

3. Stir in the barley, dill and parsley, and continue to cook until the barley grains are soft and the soup is thickened, about 20 minutes more. If mixture is very thick add a little water or broth to loosen.

4. Taste for seasoning and serve piping hot.

Information

Makes 4 servings
Each serving has 288 calories

Meatless Makeovers

21... Moussaka

This Greek favorite with a hint of spice and a burst of fresh herbs gets a meatless makeover with lentils replacing the usual lamb or beef.

Ingredients

- 1 large eggplant, peeled and cut into ½-inch slices
- Salt and pepper to taste
- 2 tbsp. olive oil
- ½ cup low-sodium vegetable broth
- 1 can (15 oz.) cooked brown lentils, drained and rinsed
- ½ cup tomato sauce
- Salt and pepper to taste
- 1 ½ tbsp. chopped fresh parsley leaves
- 1 tsp. chopped fresh thyme leaves
- 3 tbsp. Parmesan cheese
- Dash paprika

Directions

1. Preheat the oven to 350 °F.
2. Season the eggplant slices with salt and pepper. Heat the olive oil in a large non-stick skillet over medium-high heat.

3. Fry the eggplant in the oil until lightly browned and slightly softened but not cooked, about 3 minutes per side. Pour the broth around the edges of the skillet, cover, reduce the heat to low and continue to cook until eggplant is fork tender, adding a little broth to prevent sticking if necessary. Set aside

4. In a medium saucepan, combine the lentils, tomato sauce, salt, pepper, parsley, and thyme. Cook over medium heat, stirring often, until piping hot. Remove from the heat.

5. Place half the eggplant slices in the bottom of a 1-quart casserole dish. Spread the lentil mixture evenly over, and top with the remaining eggplant slices.

6. Sprinkle the Parmesan cheese over the top, add a dash of paprika, and bake in the oven until the top is golden and the edges are bubbly, 20 to 25 minutes. Serve immediately.

Information

Makes 4 servings
Each serving has 290 calories

22... Vegan Baked Rigatoni with Tofu

Tofu provides the protein while mimicking the texture of diced mozzarella in this completely vegan version of an Italian favorite.

Ingredients

- 1 (26-oz.) jar (vegan) marinara or spaghetti sauce
- 1 lb. rigatoni pasta, cooked according to pkg. directions
- 1 (15 oz.) pkg firm tofu, drained, and cut into medium cubes
- 2 tbsp. fresh basil leaves, cut into julienne
- Freshly ground black pepper
- 1 cup shredded dairy-free mozzarella cheese

Directions

1. Preheat the oven to 350 °F.

2. Spread 1/3 of the sauce in the bottom of a 9- x 13- inch casserole. Spoon half the cooked rigatoni on top and sprinkle with half the tofu and basil leaves, finishing with a grinding of black pepper.

3. Spread half the remaining sauce on top and add the remaining rigatoni, tofu, and basil as above. Finish with the remaining sauce, some black pepper, and the mozzarella cheese.

4. Bake for 30 minutes until the edges are bubbly and the cheese has melted. Remove from the oven and allow to rest for 10 minutes before serving.

Information

Makes 6 servings
Each serving has 328 calories

23... VEGETABLE GARDEN GOULASH

Traditional Hungarian goulash goes vegetarian in this sumptuous and satisfying entrée full of the goodness from the garden that great over a scoop of egg noodles.

INGREDIENTS

- 2 tbsp. olive oil
- 1 medium onion, chopped
- 1 large carrot, diced
- Salt pepper to taste
- 1 garlic clove, minced
- 2 cups low sodium vegetable broth
- 1 tbsp. Hungarian paprika
- Dash cayenne pepper
- ¾ cup no-sugar-added ketchup
- 1 ½tbsp. Worcestershire sauce
- 1 tbsp. brown sugar
- ½ tsp. dry mustard
- 1 cup diced butternut squash
- 1 medium white turnip, diced
- 8 small new potatoes
- 1 cup cauliflower florets
- ½ cup frozen peas
- 2 tbsp. all-purpose flour
- ¼ cup water

Directions

1. Heat oil over medium-high heat in a large heavy-bottomed pot. Add onion, carrot, salt and pepper and cook, stirring occasionally, for 4 minutes or until vegetables are somewhat softened.

2. Add garlic and cook a further minute. Pour in vegetable broth and bring to a simmer.

3. Add paprika, cayenne, ketchup, Worcestershire, brown sugar, and mustard and stir well to combine. Simmer for 2 minutes.

4. Add squash, turnip, and potatoes, stir well and cover. Cook on medium-low heat for 12 minutes or until vegetables are nearly fork tender, stirring occasionally.

5. Remove lid and stir in cauliflower and peas. Continue to cook until all vegetables are tender, about 5 minutes more. Stir to prevent sticking.

6. Whisk together flour and water and pour into goulash while stirring. Increase heat to medium-high and bring to a low boil. Stir constantly for 1 to 2 minutes or until mixture is very thick.

7. Remove from heat, taste for seasoning, and serve immediately over noodles, if desired.

Information

Makes 6 servings
Each serving has 255 calories

24... Oven Baked Vegetarian Paella

Here's a delicious and simply prepared paella version made with healthy brown rice and plenty of vegetables.

Ingredients

- 1 tbsp. olive oil
- 1 medium onion, chopped
- ½ medium red bell pepper, seeded and diced
- 1 large carrot, diced
- Salt and pepper to taste
- 3 garlic cloves, minced
- 2 spicy soy sausages, sliced
- 1 ½ cups long-grain brown rice
- 2 ¾ cups low-sodium vegetable broth
- 1 can (15 oz.) diced tomatoes, drained
- 1 bay leaf
- ½ tsp. crushed saffron threads
- 15 oz. extra firm tofu, diced
- 1 cup asparagus pieces, cooked to crisp tender
- ½ cup cooked edamame peas
- ½ cup frozen green peas, thawed
- 2 tsp. finely chopped fresh parsley leaves

Directions

1. Preheat the oven to 350 °F.

2. Heat the oil in a Dutch oven or other heavy-bottomed oven proof pot over medium-high heat. Add onion, bell pepper, and carrot, season with salt and pepper, and cook, stirring often, until somewhat softened, about 3 minutes. Add garlic and sausage and cook a further minute.

3. Add rice and stir to coat with onion mixture. Add broth, tomatoes, bay leaf, and saffron, and bring to a boil, stirring occasionally. Remove from heat, cover, and transfer to the oven. Cook until most of the liquid is absorbed, about 35 minutes.

4. Remove from oven, stir, and add remaining ingredients except parsley. Cover and return to oven, and cook until rice is tender, about 20 minutes.

5. Let stand, covered, for 5 minutes. Sprinkle with parsley, and serve immediately.

Information

Makes 4 servings
Each serving has 478 calories

25...Vegetarian "Veal" Parmesan

A popular Italian entrée gets a makeover with tofu and a kicked up sauce and presentation in this delicious entrée.

Ingredients

- 1 tsp. olive oil
- 1 medium zucchini, halved lengthwise and sliced
- Salt and pepper to taste
- 1 ½ cups light marinara sauce
- 1 cup artichoke hearts
- 4 (4 oz) slices extra firm tofu, patted dry
- 1 large egg, beaten
- 1 cup wholegrain or whole wheat breadcrumbs
- ¼ cup grated Parmesan cheese
- 2 tbsp. vegetable oil
- 2 cups reduced fat shredded mozzarella cheese

Directions

1. Preheat the oven to 350 °F.

2. Heat olive oil in a large skillet over medium heat, add zucchini, season with salt and pepper, and cook, stirring often, until softened and lightly browned, about 4 minutes. Add marinara sauce and artichoke hearts and continue to cook until heated through, about 3 minutes. Set aside.

3. Season both sides of tofu slices with salt and pepper.

4. Place beaten egg in a shallow bowl. Stir together breadcrumbs and cheese in another shallow bowl. Dip tofu, one at a time, into egg, allow excess to drip off, and dredge in breadcrumb mixture. Place coated cutlets on a sheet of waxed paper.

5. Heat vegetable oil in a large nonstick skillet over medium-high heat and fry tofu cutlets until golden brown, about 3 minutes per side. Transfer to a large baking dish.

6. Spoon marinara sauce with vegetables evenly over the cutlets, sprinkle mozzarella on top, and bake until sauce is bubbly and cheese has melted, 15 to 20 minutes. Serve immediately.

Information

Makes 4 servings
Each serving has 428 calories

26...Spicy Sausage and Peppers

Feel the heat as you tuck into this hearty main course featuring hot soy Italian sausage and plenty of peppers.

Ingredients

- 2 tbsp. olive oil
- 6 hot Italian style soy sausages
- 2 medium onions, sliced
- 2 medium green bell peppers, seeded and sliced
- 1 medium red or yellow bell pepper, seeded and sliced
- Salt and pepper to taste
- 4 garlic cloves, chopped
- 1 (15 oz) can tomato sauce
- 1 cup water
- 1 tsp each dried oregano, basil, and parsley
- 1 medium red-skinned potato, unpeeled and cubed

Directions

1. Heat oil in a large heavy-bottomed pot over medium-high heat. Cut sausages into bite-sized pieces and sauté in the oil until lightly browned on all sides, about 3 minutes. Remove sausages and set aside.

2. Add onions and bell peppers to pot, season with salt and pepper, and sauté, stirring often, until somewhat softened, about 5 minutes. Add garlic and cook a further minute.

3. Stir in tomato sauce, water, and dried herbs, increase heat to high and bring to a boil. Return sausages to the pot. Add potato, reduce heat to medium-low, cover, and cook at a simmer until vegetables are tender, about 20 minutes.

Information

Makes 4 servings
Each serving has 370 calories

27... Where's the "Beef" Stroganoff

An unbelievably rich and creamy sauce engulfs tender strips of tempeh in this comforting entrée that's great over brown rice or egg noodles.

Ingredients

- 1 tbsp. olive oil
- 1 lb. tempeh cut into ½-inch strips
- 1 medium onion, diced
- 1 package (10 oz) white mushrooms, wiped clean, stemmed, and halved
- 1 cup tomato sauce
- 1 cup low-sodium vegetable broth
- ½ cup low fat plain Greek yogurt
- ¼ cup fat free half and half
- Salt and pepper to taste

Directions

1. Heat the olive oil in a large non-stick skillet over medium-high heat. Add the tempeh, season with salt and pepper, and cook, stirring occasionally, until lightly browned, about 3 minutes. Remove with a slotted spoon and set aside.

2. Add the onion to the skillet and cook, stirring often, until softened, about 3 minutes.

3. Add the mushrooms to the skillet and cook 2 minutes more.

4. Stir in the tomato sauce and broth, bring to a boil, add the browned tempeh, and reduce the heat to low. Cook, covered, stirring occasionally, about 20 minutes.

5. Use a slotted spoon to transfer the tempeh and mushrooms to a warm serving bowl. Remove the skillet from the heat and add the yogurt and half and half. Whisk well to combine.

6. Taste the sauce for seasoning and pour over the tempeh and mushrooms. Serve with the egg noodles, if desired.

Information

Makes 4 servings
Each serving has 410 calories

28... Vegan Stuffed Peppers

An old favorite gets a vegan makeover in this tangy entrée featuring sweet bell peppers and tender rice, all engulfed in a savory and satisfying sauce.

Ingredients

- 2 large green bell peppers, halved, cored and seeded
- 2 tsp. olive oil
- 4 oz tempeh, crumbled
- 1 small onion, minced
- Salt and pepper to taste
- 1 garlic clove, minced
- 2 cups cooked long grain brown rice
- 1 tsp. dried parsley
- 1 cup tomato sauce
- ½ cup low-sodium vegetable broth
- ¼ cup soy milk
- Dash paprika

Directions

1. Bring a medium pot of water to the boil. Drop in the bell pepper halves and cook for 2 minutes, then remove with a slotted spoon and place on paper towels to dry. Place cut side up in a 9 x 13-inch casserole. Preheat the oven to 350 °F.

2. Heat the olive oil in a medium nonstick skillet over medium-high heat and add the tempeh, onion, salt, and pepper. Cook, stirring often, until onion is softened.

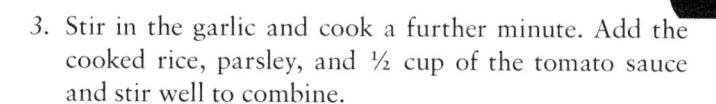

3. Stir in the garlic and cook a further minute. Add the cooked rice, parsley, and ½ cup of the tomato sauce and stir well to combine.

4. Remove from the heat and spoon the rice mixture into the bell pepper halves, pressing firmly into mounds.

5. Pour the remaining tomato sauce, broth and soymilk into the skillet and whisk to combine. Cook over low heat until just bubbly and pour evenly over the stuffed peppers.

6. Add a dash of paprika, cover the casserole with foil, and bake until the peppers are fork tender and the stuffing is piping hot, about 30 minutes. Serve immediately.

Information

Makes 4 servings
Each serving has 235 calorie

Pasta and Noodles

29...Pasta and Fagioli

The Italian definition of comfort in a bowl, this quick version of a classic is hearty, flavorful, and satisfying. Serve up with a large tossed green salad.

Ingredients

- 2 tsp. olive oil
- 1 small onion, minced
- 1 small celery stalk, finely chopped
- 1 small carrot, cut into small dice
- Salt and pepper to taste
- 1 garlic clove, minced
- ½ cup low-sodium vegetable broth
- 1 can (8 oz.) tomato sauce
- 1 can (15 oz.) vegetarian beans in sauce, undrained (such as Heinz or Campbell's)
- 8 oz. ditalini pasta, cooked according to package directions
- Extra virgin olive oil for drizzling

Directions

1. Heat oil in a large pot over medium-high heat. Add onion, celery, carrot, salt and pepper, and cook, stirring often, until softened, about 5 minutes. Add garlic and cook a further minute.

Pasta and noodles

2. Stir in broth and tomato sauce and bring to a low boil, stirring often. Add beans and pasta and cook, over medium heat, until heated through and bubbly, about 3 minutes. Stir often to prevent sticking.

3. Season with salt and pepper and serve in large bowls with a drizzle of extra virgin olive oil.

Information

Makes 4 servings
Each serving has 350 calories

30...Penne with Sun-Dried Tomato Pesto

Both sweet and sharp tasting, sun-dried tomato pesto is the perfect foil for whole wheat pasta and making your own version of pesto allows for fewer calories and a lot less added fat.

Ingredients

- 1 cup drained oil-packed sun-dried tomatoes
- 1/3 cup torn fresh basil leaves
- 2 tbsp. slivered almonds
- 2 garlic cloves
- ¼ cup extra virgin olive oil
- ¼ cup grated Parmesan cheese plus more for sprinkling
- 12 oz. whole wheat penne pasta
- ¼ cup fat free half and half
- Salt and pepper to taste

Directions

1. Bring a large pot of water to boil over high heat.
2. Combine sun-dried tomatoes, basil, almonds and garlic in a food processor and pulse until chopped. While processor is running, slowly add olive oil until a paste is formed. Transfer to a bowl and stir in Parmesan cheese.

3. Cook pasta according to package directions, reserve ½ cup of cooking liquid, and drain. Add pesto to pot and stir together with reserved liquid. Return pasta to pot, add half and half, and toss well to coat.

4. Season with salt and pepper and serve with a sprinkle of Parmesan cheese.

Information

Makes 4 servings
Each serving has 415 calories
For Vegan: substitute soy creamer or soy milk for half and half

31...Spinach Spaghetti Puttanesca

Named after the ladies of the night, this dish is spicy, bold, and deliciously alluring, made here without the typical addition of anchovies and a switch to spinach pasta for added nutrition and fiber.

Ingredients

- 2 tbsp. olive oil
- 4 garlic cloves, sliced
- 1 can (15 oz.) crushed tomatoes
- ½ cup pitted Kalamata olives, roughly chopped
- 2 tbsp. drained small capers
- ¼ tsp. red pepper flakes
- Pinch sugar
- 12 oz. spinach spaghetti or linguine
- Salt and pepper to taste
- 2 tbsp. roughly chopped fresh Italian parsley leaves

Directions

1. Bring a large pot of salted water to boil over high heat.

2. Heat olive oil in a large non-stick skillet over medium-high heat. Add garlic and cook, stirring often, for 1 minute. Add crushed tomatoes, olives, capers, red pepper flakes, and sugar, and allow to simmer over medium-low heat, stirring occasionally, until thickened, about 15 minutes.

3. Cook spaghetti according to package directions, drain, and return to the hot pot. Add cooked tomato sauce and toss well to coat. Season with salt and pepper and serve immediately sprinkled with parsley.

INFORMATION

Makes 4 servings
Each serving has 385 calories

32...Harvest Whole Wheat Lasagne

The intense, sweet flavor of roasted butternut squash pairs well with creamy ricotta and nutty whole wheat lasagna in this easy version of a pasta favorite.

Ingredients

- 2 cups butternut squash, cut into ½-inch dice
- 1 tbsp. olive oil
- 1 tsp. dried oregano
- Salt and pepper to taste
- 1 container (15 oz.) part skim ricotta cheese
- 1 large egg, lightly beaten
- 2 tbsp. grated Parmesan cheese
- Dash ground nutmeg
- 1 jar (28 oz.) light marinara or spaghetti sauce
- 9 pieces (8 oz.) whole wheat lasagna, cooked according to package directions, drained and rinsed under cold water
- 1 cup reduced fat shredded mozzarella cheese

Directions

1. Preheat the oven to 375 °F. Combine squash, olive oil, oregano, salt and pepper in a medium bowl and toss well. Transfer to a large baking sheet with a rim, spread out evenly, and roast in the oven, stirring occasionally, until tender and lightly golden, about 15 minutes.

2. In a medium bowl stir together ricotta cheese, egg, Parmesan, nutmeg, and salt and pepper to taste.

3. Spread ¼ of the marinara sauce on the bottom of a 9 x 13-inch casserole and place 3 lasagna noodles in a single layer over sauce. Spread half of ricotta mixture over lasagna, and distribute half roasted butternut squash on top. Spread 1/3 of the remaining sauce over squash and sprinkle with 1/3 of mozzarella cheese. Top with 3 lasagna noodles and repeat.

4. Cover top noodles with remaining sauce and mozzarella, and bake until bubbly around the edges and the cheese has melted, about 35 minutes. Let rest 10 minutes before slicing and serving.

Information

Makes 6 servings
Each serving has 348 calories

33...Linguine with Broccoli Rabe and Tempeh

The bold flavors of broccoli rabe and garlic are the perfect complement to earthy tempeh and hearty wholegrain linguine.

Ingredients

- 1 tbsp. olive oil
- 1 cup crumbled tempeh
- 2 garlic cloves, sliced
- 1 bunch broccoli rabe, cleaned and trimmed of hard stems
- Salt and pepper to taste
- 2/3 cup low sodium vegetable broth
- 8 oz. wholegrain linguine or spaghetti
- ¼ cup grated Romano cheese plus more for sprinkling

Directions

1. Bring a large pot of salted water to the boil.
2. In a large non-stick skillet heat the oil over medium-high heat, add the tempeh and cook, stirring often, until lightly browned, about 3 minutes. Add garlic and cook a further minute.
3. Add broccoli rabe, season with salt and pepper, and cook, stirring often, for 2 minutes. Add broth, bring to a boil, cover and reduce heat to low. Cook until broccoli rabe is fork tender yet firm, about 8 minutes.

4. Meanwhile cook linguine according to package directions. Drain and add to skillet with sausage and broccoli rabe. Add Romano cheese, and toss well to combine. Serve immediately with additional Romano for sprinkling.

Information

Makes 4 servings
Each serving has 390 calories

34...Best Ever Baked Ziti

Delicious morsels of tender eggplant and creamy dollops of goat cheese replace the meat in this healthy version made with whole wheat pasta.

Ingredients

- 2 tbsp. olive oil
- 1 medium eggplant, peeled and cut into 1-inch dice
- Salt and pepper to taste
- ½ cup water
- 2 tbsp. chopped fresh basil leaves
- 1 jar (28 oz.) light marinara or spaghetti sauce
- 1 log (3 oz.) goat cheese, cut into small chunks
- 12 oz. whole wheat or wholegrain ziti (or penne), cooked according to package directions
- 1 cup reduced fat shredded mozzarella cheese

Directions

1. Preheat the oven to 350 °F.

2. Heat oil in a large nonstick skillet over medium-high heat. Add eggplant, season with salt and pepper, and sauté quickly just to lightly brown but not cook, stirring often, about 3 minutes. Pour in the water, stir and cover. Reduce the heat to low and cook, stirring occasionally, until fork tender, about 4 minutes more. Stir in basil and transfer to a 9 x 13-inch casserole.

3. Add marinara sauce, goat cheese, and cooked ziti to casserole, stirring well to combine. Top with the mozzarella cheese.

4. Bake until bubbly and cheese has melted, 25 to 30 minutes. Serve immediately.

Information

Makes 6 servings
Each serving has 430 calories
For Vegan: substitute goat cheese with a soft soy-made cheese and the mozzarella with a vegan shredded melting cheese

35...Mushroom Tortellini with Walnuts

Stuffed pasta enrobed in a creamy and flavorful sauce gets a healthy protein boost from toasted walnuts.

Ingredients

- ¼ cup walnut pieces
- 1 tbsp. olive oil
- 1 shallot, minced
- 1 garlic clove, minced
- ½ cup non-fat plain Greek style yogurt
- ¼ cup low fat milk
- Salt and pepper to taste
- 1 package (8 oz.) mushroom tortellini, cooked according to package directions
- ¼ cup reduced fat feta cheese, crumbled

Directions

1. In a large non-stick skillet, toast walnuts over high heat, shaking pan often, until fragrant and lightly browned, about 3 minutes. Transfer to a small bowl and set aside.

2. Heat olive oil in same skillet over medium-high heat, add shallot, and cook stirring occasionally, until softened, about 3 minutes. Add garlic and cook a further minute.

3. Reduce heat to low and whisk in the yogurt and milk to gently warm, being careful not to boil. Season with salt and pepper and remove from the heat.

4. Add the walnuts and hot cooked tortellini to the sauce. Stir well to coat and serve sprinkled with the feta cheese.

Information

Makes 4 servings
Each serving has 320 calories
For Vegan: substitute soy yogurt and milk for the Greek yogurt and cow's milk and top with a vegan grated or shredded parmesan-flavored cheese

36...Pumpkin Ravioli with Pepitas

Both sweet and savory, with protein and crunch from pumpkin seeds, this delectable dish is a snap to make with prepared ravioli.

Ingredients

- 1 tbsp. olive oil
- ½ medium red onion, thinly sliced
- Salt and pepper to taste
- 2 cups trimmed and washed beet tops or red chard
- ½ cup low sodium vegetable broth
- ¼ cup fat free half and half
- 1 package (8 oz.) pumpkin or butternut squash ravioli, prepared according to package directions
- ¼ cup pepitas (toasted pumpkin seeds)
- 2 tbsp. dried cranberries
- 2 tbsp. crumbled goat cheese

Directions

1. Heat oil in a large nonstick skillet over medium heat. Add red onion, sprinkle with salt and pepper, and cook, stirring occasionally, until softened, about 4 minutes.

2. Add beet tops and broth, increase heat to medium-high, and cook until greens are wilted, about 4 minutes. Add half and half, ravioli, pepitas, and cranberries, and gently toss to combine. Cook for 2 minutes, remove from heat, cover, and set aside for 2 minutes.

3. Serve topped with goat cheese.

Information

Makes 4 servings
Each serving has 215 calories
For Vegan: substitute soy creamer or soymilk for the half and half and a vegan crumbled cheese for the goat cheese

37... Gnocchi with Garlic Sautéed Broccoli

Potato gnocchi and crisp tender broccoli florets take on the zesty flavor of garlic in this tasty and satisfying entrée.

Ingredients

- 2 tbsp. olive oil
- 6 garlic cloves, minced
- Salt and pepper to taste
- 3 cups broccoli florets, par-cooked to crisp tender
- 8 oz frozen or fresh potato gnocchi, cooked according to package directions
- ¼ cup grated Romano cheese, plus more for sprinkling

Directions

1. Heat olive oil in a large nonstick skillet over medium heat. Add garlic, sprinkle with salt and pepper, and cook, stirring often, until somewhat softened but not browned, about 2 minutes.

2. Add broccoli, stir well to coat, and cook for 2 minutes more. Add gnocchi and cheese, stir to combine and continue cooking until piping hot, about 2 minutes.

3. Season with salt and pepper to taste. Serve immediately, sprinkled with more Romano cheese.

Pasta and noodles

INFORMATION

Makes 4 servings
Each serving has 290 calories

38...Farfalle and Kasha with Sweet Onions and Carrots

Here's a lightened up version of the delicious Jewish dish made with nutty toasted buckwheat (kasha) and flavorful caramelized onion and carrots.

Ingredients

- ¾ cup medium grain kasha
- 1 large egg, slightly beaten
- 1 tbsp. vegetable oil
- 1 medium onion, halved and thinly sliced
- 1 cup shredded carrots
- Salt and pepper to taste
- 1 ½ cups low-sodium vegetable broth
- 6 oz dry farfalle (bowtie) pasta, cooked according to package directions

Directions

1. Place the kasha in a medium mixing bowl and stir in the beaten egg, being sure to coat each grain.

2. Heat the vegetable oil in a large nonstick skillet over medium-high heat. Add the onions and carrots, season with the salt and pepper, and cook, stirring often, until the vegetables are softened and slightly browned, about 5 minutes.

3. Add the kasha to the skillet and, using the back of a fork, break up any clumps, and stir while cooking until the egg has dried and the kasha begins to toast, 3 to 4 minutes.

4. Pour in the broth, bring to a boil, reduce the heat to low, cover, and cook until the kasha is tender, 10 to 15 minutes.

5. Add the cooked bowties, stir to combine well, and cook a further 3 to 4 minutes until piping hot. Taste for seasoning and serve immediately.

INFORMATION

Makes 4 servings
Each serving has 335 calories

39... Vegan Stuffed Shells

Smooth and rich tofu, flavored with Italian herbs and combined with nutritious spinach, replaces the usual ricotta filling in this terrific all vegan version of an old favorite.

Ingredients

- 1 (15 oz.) package extra-firm tofu
- 1 (10 oz.) package frozen chopped spinach, cooked according to package directions and squeezed dry
- 1 tbsp. vegan parmesan cheese
- ¼ tsp. garlic salt
- 1 tsp. dried oregano
- 1 tsp. dried basil
- Salt and pepper to taste
- 2 cups prepared light marinara sauce
- 12 jumbo pasta shells, cooked according to package directions
- 1 cup shredded soy mozzarella

Directions

1. Preheat the oven to 350 °F.

2. Place the tofu, spinach, parmesan, garlic salt, oregano, and basil in a food processor fitted with a steel blade and process until smooth. Transfer to a bowl, season with salt and pepper to taste and set aside.

3. Pour half the marinara sauce into a 2 qt. casserole and spread evenly.

4. Stuff the cooked shells with the spinach mixture using a large spoon and place side by side in the casserole.

5. Evenly spread the remaining marinara sauce over the shells, cover the casserole with foil, and bake for 20 minutes.

6. Remove the foil, sprinkle the mozzarella over, and bake a further 10 minutes until the cheese has melted and the sauce is bubbly. Remove from the oven and let rest 10 minutes before serving.

INFORMATION

Makes 4 servings
Each serving has 345 calories

40... Vegan Spaghetti "Bolognese"

You'll marvel at the flavor in this easy-to-make vegan version of a popular pasta dish where tempeh replaces the meat for protein and texture.

Ingredients

- 2 tbsp. olive oil
- ½ medium onion, finely diced
- 1 medium celery stalk, diced
- 1 medium carrot, diced
- Salt and freshly ground pepper
- 1 cup tempeh, crumbled
- 1 garlic clove, minced
- 1 (28 oz) can chopped tomatoes
- 1 (8 oz.) can tomato sauce
- 2 tbsp. tomato paste
- Pinch granulated sugar
- 2 tsp. dried oregano
- 2 tsp. dried basil
- 1 tsp. dried parsley
- Dash crushed red pepper flakes
- 1 bay leaf
- 8 oz. spaghetti, preferably whole grain, cooked according to package directions
- Vegan parmesan cheese for sprinkling

Directions

1. Heat oil in a heavy bottomed pot over medium-high heat. Add onion, celery, and carrot, season with salt and pepper, and cook, stirring often, for 3 minutes or until softened. Do not brown. Add tempeh and continue to cook, browning slightly, about 2 minutes.

2. Add garlic and cook a further minute.

3. Stir in tomatoes, tomato sauce, paste, sugar, oregano, basil, parsley, red pepper flakes, and bay leaf. Bring to a simmer over medium-high heat, stirring often. Reduce to very low and allow to cook at a low simmer for 20 minutes or until flavorful and thickened.

4. Serve immediately over spaghetti with a sprinkling of cheese.

Information

Makes 4 servings
Each serving has 458 calories

41...Plum-Glazed Tofu and Rice Noodles

Calcium rich and protein packed, this Asian-style dish flavored with sweet do-it-yourself plum sauce and sharp ginger is a delicious and satisfying entrée.

Ingredients

- 1 lb. extra-firm tofu, halved and cut into 16 slices
- Salt and pepper to taste
- 1 tbsp. vegetable oil
- ½ red bell pepper, cored, seeded and sliced
- 1 bunch scallions, trimmed and cut into 2-inch pieces
- ½ cup sliced water chestnuts, drained
- ½ cup low sodium vegetable broth
- 6 oz. medium-wide rice noodles, cooked according to package directions, tossed with a drizzle of sesame oil

For the Plum Sauce:

- ½ cup no-sugar-added plum jam
- 1 tbsp. finely chopped fresh ginger
- 1 tbsp. lemon juice
- 1 tsp. soy sauce

Directions

1. Press the tofu slices between paper towels to remove all excess liquid. Season with salt and pepper.

2. In a large non-stick skillet or wok, heat the oil over high heat. Carefully place the tofu slices in the skillet and brown lightly, 1 to 2 minutes per side. Remove with a spatula and set aside.

3. Add the bell pepper and scallions to the skillet and cook, stirring constantly over high heat until somewhat softened, about 2 minutes. Add the water chestnuts and cook a further minute.

4. Pour in the broth, return the tofu slices to the skillet, cover and cook on low for 2 minutes.

5. Meanwhile, in a small bowl make the plum sauce by stirring together the plum jam, ginger, lemon juice, and soy sauce.

6. Remove the lid and add the plum sauce. Gently stir tofu and vegetables to coat. Cook 1 to 2 minutes more until thick and bubbly. Transfer to a bowl and serve immediately on top of the rice noodles.

Information

Makes 4 servings
Each serving has 398 calories

42...Pad Thai Noodle Wraps

Hot and spicy, you'll love these Thai-inspired wraps fragrant with cilantro and deliciously satisfying with a sprinkling of roasted peanuts.

Ingredients

- 8 oz. thin rice noodles, cooked according to package directions
- 1 tbsp. vegetable oil
- 1 large garlic clove, minced
- ¼ cup unseasoned rice vinegar
- 2 tbsp. light agave nectar
- 3 tbsp. tomato sauce
- 1 tbsp. soy sauce
- 1 tbsp. Thai chili sauce, or to taste
- 1 tbsp. lime juice
- 2/3 cup shredded carrots
- 1 cup snow peas, thinly sliced
- 3 scallions, trimmed and cut into 2-inch pieces
- 1 ½ cups fresh bean sprouts
- Salt and pepper to taste
- 3 tbsp. chopped fresh cilantro leaves
- 2 tbsp. chopped lightly salted roasted peanuts
- 8 large lettuce leaves for wrapping

Directions

1. Heat oil in a large nonstick skillet over medium-high heat. Add garlic and cook, stirring, 1 minute.

2. Add cooked rice noodles and stir fry for 2 minutes or until heated through.

3. In a small bowl whisk together vinegar, agave, tomato sauce, soy sauce, chili sauce, and lime juice. Pour over noodles and cook 3 minutes, stirring often, until noodles are completely transparent.

4. Add carrots, snow peas, scallions, and bean sprouts and stir fry for 2 to 3 minutes until heated through. Season with salt and pepper and remove from heat.

5. Mound noodle mixture into center of lettuce leaves, sprinkle with cilantro and peanuts, and roll up to serve.

Information

Makes 4 servings
Each serving has 289 calories

43...Divine Noodle Kugel

This slightly sweet, creamy and rich Jewish holiday dish becomes a healthy meal in itself for vegetarian diners, with a hint of cinnamon and the natural sweetness of golden raisins.

Ingredients

- 8 oz. medium egg noodles
- ½ cup low fat plain Greek yogurt
- ½ cup low fat cottage cheese
- 3 tbsp. reduced fat cream cheese
- ¼ cup granulated sugar substitute
- 1 large egg
- 1 large egg white
- ½ tsp. vanilla
- ¼ tsp. ground cinnamon
- 2/3 cup golden raisins

Directions

1. Cook egg noodles according to package directions. Drain, rinse under cold water, and set aside.

2. Preheat the oven to 350 °F. Lightly coat the bottom and sides of a 2 quart casserole dish with cooking spray.

3. In a large mixing bowl, using an electric mixer, beat together yogurt, cottage cheese, cream cheese, and sugar until smooth. Add egg, egg white, vanilla, and cinnamon and beat for 2 minutes or until well combined.

4. Add raisins and drained noodles and stir well to distribute cheese mixture. Transfer to the prepared casserole and smooth out evenly.

5. Bake for 30 to 35 minutes or until the top is lightly browned and the kugel is firmly set.

6. Cool slightly on a wire rack before cutting and serving.

INFORMATION

Makes 4 servings
Each serving has 370 calories

Pizzas and Sandwiches

44... Week Night Thin Crust Pizza

Making use of pre-baked crusts will put dinner on the table in no time as in this delicious whole wheat version topped with classic Italian ingredients.

Ingredients

- 1 8-inch whole wheat thin crust pizza
- ¼ cup marinara sauce
- ¼ cup reduced fat shredded mozzarella cheese
- 1 plum tomato, thinly sliced
- Pinch dried oregano
- Fresh basil leaves, torn
- Drizzle extra virgin olive oil

Directions

1. Preheat oven to 450 °F or according to crust package directions.
2. Place pre-baked pizza crust on a work surface and spread marinara sauce on top. Sprinkle with mozzarella, and distribute tomato slices around evenly. Sprinkle the oregano over.
3. Bake until pizza is crisp and cheese has melted, 8 to 10 minutes. Transfer pizza with metal spatulas to a cutting board and top with the basil and olive oil. Slice and serve.

Pizzas and sandwiches

INFORMATION

Makes 1 serving
Each serving has 430 calories

45...Autumn Delight Pizza

The ingredients reminiscent of fall come together in this healthy pizza that gets added flavor from smoked cheese.

Ingredients

- 1 8-inch whole wheat thin crust pizza
- 2/3 cup roasted diced butternut or acorn squash
- ¼ cup reduced fat smoked Gouda or mozzarella cheese
- 1 tbsp. golden raisins
- 1 tbsp. walnut pieces
- 1 tsp. chopped fresh parsley leaves
- Dollops of nonfat plain Greek yogurt
- 1 tsp. maple syrup or agave nectar

Directions

1. Preheat oven to 450 °F or according to directions.
2. Place pre-baked pizza crust on a work surface and spread squash on top. Sprinkle with the cheese, raisins, nuts, and parsley.
3. Bake until pizza is crisp and cheese has melted, 8 to 10 minutes. Transfer pizza with metal spatulas to a cutting board and top with the yogurt and maple syrup.

Information

Makes 1 serving
Each serving has 445 calories

Pizzas and sandwiches

46...Broccoli and Ricotta Pizza

Delicious garlic flavored broccoli stars in this simple and easy to make pizza that's super satisfying.

Ingredients

- 1 8-inch whole wheat thin crust pizza
- ½ cup part-skim ricotta cheese
- 1 cup small broccoli florets, cooked to crisp tender
- 1 tsp. olive oil
- 1 small garlic clove, minced
- Salt and pepper to taste
- 1 tbsp. shredded Parmesan cheese

Directions

1. Preheat oven to 450 °F or according to directions.

2. Place pre-baked pizza crust on a work surface and spread ricotta on top. In a small bowl toss together the broccoli, olive oil, garlic, and salt and pepper, and distribute over the ricotta.

3. Sprinkle the Parmesan over and bake until pizza is crisp and cheese has melted, 8 to 10 minutes. Transfer pizza with metal spatulas to a cutting board, slice and serve.

Information

Makes 1 serving
Each serving has 390 calories

47... Greek Salad Pita Pizza

You'll enjoy two dishes in one with this healthy light supper idea that's full of the great flavors of the Aegean.

Ingredients

- 1 ½ cups salad greens
- 3 cherry tomatoes, halved
- ¼ cup diced cucumber
- ¼ cup shaved red onion
- ¼ cup thinly sliced green bell pepper
- 2 tbsp. pitted Kalamata olives
- 2 tsp. olive oil
- Salt and pepper to taste
- Lemon juice to taste
- Pinch dried oregano
- 1 large whole wheat pita
- 3 tbsp. crumbled reduced fat feta cheese

Directions

1. Preheat the oven to 425 °F.

2. In a large mixing bowl toss together the greens, tomatoes, cucumber, onion, bell pepper, and olives. In a small bowl whisk together the olive oil, salt, pepper, lemon juice, and oregano and set aside.

3. Place the pita on a pizza stone or hot baking sheet and sprinkle the feta over. Bake just until the edges begin to brown and the cheese has melted, 8 to 10 minutes.

Pizzas and sandwiches

4. Meanwhile toss together the dressing and the salad ingredients. When the pita is ready, transfer to a large serving plate and mound the salad on top. Serve immediately.

Information

Makes 1 serving
Each serving has 440 calories

48...Grilled Vegetable Pizza

Use your leftover grilled veggies for a quick dinner solution with this deliciously simple idea.

Ingredients

- 1 8-inch whole wheat thin crust pizza
- Olive oil for brushing
- 1 large garlic clove, smashed
- Assorted grilled vegetables such as eggplant, peppers, onions, asparagus, or zucchini
- 1 oz goat cheese, diced

Directions

1. Heat grill to medium high or preheat the oven to 450 °F.

2. Lightly brush the pizza crust with olive oil and toast on the grill (or oven rack) for a few minutes on both sides. Rub the garlic clove over the top and discard.

3. Layer the vegetables on top and sprinkle the goat cheese over. Return to the grill on medium heat, close the lid, and cook until the veggies are heated through and the cheese has begun to melt, about 3 minutes.

4. Serve sprinkled with the fresh herbs.

Information

Makes 1 serving   Each serving has 380 calories

49... Whole Grain Open Face Veggie Club

Start with a fiber-rich grain bread and you're well on your way to a healthy and delicious take on a classic sandwich that's perfect with a cup of soup for a quick light supper.

Ingredients

- 1 (½-inch thick) slice whole grain bread
- ¼ ripe avocado, mashed
- 1 thin slice reduced fat cheese
- 1 hard cooked egg, peeled and sliced
- Salt and pepper to taste
- Sliced tomato
- Handful alfalfa or clover sprouts

Directions

1. Toast the bread and place on a cutting board. Spread the avocado over.

2. Top with the remaining ingredients in order listed, and using a serrated knife, cut in half and transfer to a plate. Serve immediately.

Information

Makes 1 serving
Each serving has 370 calories

50...Bean and Artichoke Panini

Ingredients

- 2 tbsp. pitted Sicilian, or large green olives, roughly chopped
- 1 tsp. small capers
- 1 small garlic clove, minced
- 2 tbsp. diced celery
- 1 tbsp. light mayonnaise
- 1 tsp. fresh lemon juice
- ¼ cup marinated artichokes, drained and roughly chopped
- ½ cup canned cannellini beans, drained and rinsed
- 1 tbsp. coarsely chopped Italian parsley
- Freshly ground pepper to taste
- 1 small whole wheat crusty roll

Directions

1. In a small bowl stir together olives, capers, garlic, celery, mayonnaise, and lemon juice.
2. In a medium bowl toss together artichokes, cannellini beans, parsley, and pepper.
3. Slice open the roll horizontally. Spread mayonnaise mixture evenly on cut sides, and fill with bean mixture.

Information

Makes 1 serving
Serving has 375 calories

Pizzas and sandwiches

51... Curry Tofu Salad Pita Pockets

Almonds, pineapple, and curry add crunch and flavor to this delicious vegetarian version of a traditional chicken salad favorite.

Ingredients

- 1 cup diced extra-firm tofu
- ¼ tsp. curry powder
- Dash paprika
- Salt and pepper to taste
- 2 tbsp. coarsely chopped almonds
- ¼ cup diced fresh or canned pineapple, drained, juices reserved
- 1 small celery stalk, diced
- ¼ cup plain low fat Greek yogurt
- 1 tbsp. pineapple juice
- 1 whole wheat pita, cut in half and opened

Directions

1. In a medium bowl combine tofu, curry powder, paprika, salt, pepper, almonds, pineapple, and celery and toss to combine. Add yogurt and pineapple juice and gently stir to coat.

2. Stuff each pita half with the salad and serve immediately.

Information

Makes 1 serving
Serving has 368 calories

52...Hummus and Greek Salad Wrap

Enjoy this Mediterranean salad wrap that's surprisingly hearty and filling for a light supper with a cup of soup.

Ingredients

- 1 medium multigrain or whole wheat wrap
- ½ cup prepared hummus
- ½ small tomato, diced
- ¼ cup diced green bell pepper
- ¼ cup diced red onion
- ¼ cup shredded carrot
- ¼ cup shredded red cabbage
- 1 tbsp. light bottled olive oil and vinegar dressing

Directions

1. Place wrap on a cutting board and spread hummus in center third to the edges.
2. Top evenly with the remaining ingredients and drizzle the dressing evenly over.
3. Make wrap by folding edges in 1 inch, then rolling wrap up and away from you. Cut in half and serve immediately.

Information

Makes 1 serving
Serving has 315 calories

Pizzas and sandwiches

53...Grilled Eggplant and Mozzarella Burger

Get rave results from even the staunchest of meat eaters.

Ingredients

- Olive oil for grilling
- 8 (½-inch) eggplant slices
- Salt and pepper to taste
- 4 (¼-inch) mozzarella slices
- 4 sun-dried tomatoes, thinly sliced
- 4 large fresh basil leaves
- 4 light whole wheat burger buns, toasted

Directions

1. Heat an outdoor or indoor grill to medium high and coat lightly with olive oil. Grill eggplant slices, seasoning with salt and pepper and brushing on additional oil, until tender, turning occasionally, about 10 minutes.
2. While still on the grill, top 4 eggplant slices with cheese, sun-dried tomatoes, and basil leaves and place remaining eggplant slices on top. Press down gently with a spatula and continue grilling until cheese melts.
3. Transfer to toasted buns and serve immediately.

Information

Makes 4 servings
Each serving has 320 calories

Rice, Grains and Beans

54...Cajun Red Beans and Rice

The spicy and seductive flavors of Louisiana beckon in this hearty rendition of a Southern classic.

Ingredients

- 1 tbsp. olive oil
- 1 medium onion, chopped
- 1 medium green bell pepper, seeded and chopped
- 1 medium celery stalk, chopped
- 2 garlic cloves, minced
- 1 tsp. Cajun or Creole seasoning
- 1 cup low-sodium vegetable broth
- 1 can (15 oz) Roma tomatoes, roughly chopped
- 2 cans (15 oz.) red beans or kidney beans, drained and rinsed
- Salt and pepper to taste
- 2 cups cooked long grain brown rice

Directions

1. Heat oil in a large nonstick skillet over medium-high heat. Add onion, bell pepper, and celery and cook, stirring often, until softened, about 8 minutes. Stir in garlic and Cajun seasoning and cook a further minute.

2. Add broth and tomatoes, bring to a simmer, and cook stirring occasionally for 5 minutes. Stir in beans and continue cooking until creamy and piping hot, about 10 minutes more. Season to taste with salt and pepper.

3. Serve immediately ladled over the hot rice.

INFORMATION

Makes 4 servings
Each serving has 415 calories

55...Lentil and Couscous Curry

Tender couscous pairs with protein-rich lentils in this flavorful exotic dish with hints of curry and cinnamon.

Ingredients

- 3 cups low-sodium vegetable broth
- 1 tsp. curry powder
- ½ tsp. ground turmeric
- ½ cup red lentils, picked over and rinsed
- 1 cup dry couscous, preferably whole wheat
- 1/3 cup currants or raisins
- 1/3 cup frozen peas, thawed
- 1 cinnamon stick
- ¼ cup sliced almonds
- 4 green onions, thinly sliced
- Salt and pepper to taste

Directions

1. In a medium saucepan bring broth to the boil. Stir in curry powder, turmeric and lentils, reduce heat to low, cover and cook until tender, 25 to 30 minutes.

2. Add couscous, currants and peas, and stir well to combine. Place cinnamon on top, cover and remove from heat. Let stand for 10 minutes.

3. Fluff couscous mixture with a fork and gently stir in almonds and green onions. Season with salt and pepper and serve immediately.

Rice, grains and beans

INFORMATION

Makes 4 servings
Each serving has 310 calories

56... Ratatouille Quinoa Casserole

The herbs of Provence waft through the kitchen as this delectable, colorful casserole bakes and bubbles.

Ingredients

- 1 tbsp. olive oil
- 2 cups cooked quinoa
- 2 medium zucchini, cut into ½-inch rounds
- 1 medium yellow squash, cut into ½-inch rounds
- 1 large green bell pepper, seeded and cut into 1-inch pieces
- 2 small red onions, cut into ¼-inch rounds
- 2 small eggplant, left unpeeled and cut into ½-inch rounds
- 4 plum tomatoes, cut into ½-inch rounds
- Salt and pepper to taste
- 2 tsp. Herbes de Provence
- ½ cup low-sodium vegetable broth
- ½ cup whole wheat or wholegrain bread crumbs

Directions

1. Preheat the oven to 350 °F. Lightly coat a shallow oval or rectangular 1½ quart baking dish with 1 teaspoon of olive oil. Spread the quinoa evenly over the bottom.

2. Layer the vegetables in rows, domino fashion, staggering them to distribute the different vegetables throughout. Season with salt and pepper and sprinkle the herbs over.

Rice, grains and beans

3. Pour vegetable broth on top and drizzle the remaining olive oil over the top. Lightly press bread crumbs over top of casserole to cover vegetables.

4. Bake until vegetables are fork tender, most of liquid has evaporated, and crumb topping is golden, about 40 minutes. Allow to rest for 10 minutes before serving.

Information

Makes 4 servings
Each serving has 320 calories

57...Risotto with Cabbage and Chickpeas

Hearty and full of flavor, risotto goes country-style with cabbage and beans in this delicious version enhanced with the tang of lemon zest.

Ingredients

- 6 large Savoy cabbage leaves, hard centers removed
- 1 tbsp. olive oil
- 1 tsp. unsalted butter
- 3 shallots, finely chopped
- Salt and pepper to taste
- 1 ½ cups Arborio rice
- 1 quart low-sodium vegetable broth, kept hot on the back burner
- ½ cup canned chickpeas, drained and rinsed
- 1/3 cup canned cannellini beans, drained and rinsed
- 1 tsp. grated lemon zest
- ¼ cup grated Parmesan cheese

Directions

- Bring a medium pot of salted water to the boil. Submerge cabbage leaves and cook for 5 minutes. Drain, rinse under cold water, pat dry, and roughly chop. Set aside.
- Heat butter and olive oil in a large saucepan over medium heat. Add shallots and chopped cabbage, season with salt and pepper, and cook, stirring, until softened, about 3 minutes. Do not brown.

Rice, grains and beans

- Add rice and cook, stirring constantly, for 1 minute.
- Using a ½ cup ladle, begin adding hot broth to rice, stirring constantly each time, until liquid has been absorbed. Be sure to keep rice at a low simmer while stirring. When about ½ cup broth remains, stir in chickpeas and cannellini beans.
- Add remaining broth and cook, stirring, until rice is tender and creamy but still firm to the bite. The rice should require about 25 minutes of cooking from beginning to end.
- Remove from heat and stir in lemon zest and Parmesan. Season to taste with salt and pepper, and serve immediately.

INFORMATION

Makes 4 servings
Each serving has 335 calories
For Vegan: substitute dairy-free margarine for butter and vegan grated parmesan-style cheese for Parmesan

58...Mushroom Medley Barley Risotto

Nutty barley takes the place of rice, adding protein and fiber, in this earthy mushroom and herb flavored risotto.

Ingredients

- 1 tbsp. olive oil
- 1 tsp. unsalted butter
- 1 small onion, finely chopped
- 10 oz. wild mushrooms, sliced
- 1 large Portobello mushroom, stem and gills removed, cap chopped
- Salt and pepper to taste
- 1 large garlic clove, minced
- 2 tbsp. chopped fresh parsley
- 2 tsp. chopped fresh thyme
- 1 tsp. chopped fresh sage
- 1 cup pearl barley
- 5 cups low sodium vegetable broth
- ¼ cup fat free half and half
- ¼ cup grated Parmesan cheese

Rice, grains and beans

Directions

1. Heat oil and butter in a heavy large saucepan over medium heat. Add onion and cook, stirring often, until softened, about 3 minutes. Add sliced mushrooms and chopped Portobello, season with salt and pepper, and cook, stirring occasionally, until lightly golden, about 10 minutes.

2. Stir in garlic, parsley, thyme, and sage, and cook for 2 minutes. Add barley, stir well to coat, and cook a further minute.

3. Add 4 cups of broth and bring to a boil. Reduce heat to medium-low, cover, and cook until liquid is nearly absorbed, about 30 minutes.

4. Stir half and half into remaining broth and add to saucepan with barley. Continue to cook, uncovered, stirring often, until barley is tender and mixture is creamy, about 10 minutes.

5. Remove from heat, stir in Parmesan, season with salt and pepper, and serve immediately.

Information

Makes 4 servings
Each serving has 375 calories
For Vegan: substitute dairy-free margarine for butter, soy creamer or soymilk for half and half, and vegan parmesan style grated cheese for Parmesan

59...Brown Rice and Butternut Risotto

Creamy and sweet butternut squash takes center stage in this healthy rendition made with aromatic brown rice.

Ingredients

- 1 tbsp. olive oil
- 1 small onion, finely chopped
- 1 garlic clove, minced
- 1 cup brown Arborio or short grain rice
- ¼ cup apple juice
- 6 cups low sodium vegetable broth, kept hot on the back burner
- 1 small butternut squash, peeled, seeded and cut into ½-inch dice
- ¼ cup chopped hazelnuts
- 1 tbsp. chopped fresh basil
- 1 tsp. dried oregano
- 1 tsp. unsalted butter
- ¼ cup grated Parmesan cheese
- Salt and pepper to taste
- ¼ cup reduced fat feta cheese, crumbled

Directions

1. Heat olive oil in a heavy medium saucepan over medium heat. Add onion and cook, stirring often, until softened, about 3 minutes. Add garlic and cook a further minute.

2. Add rice and cook, stirring constantly, for 1 minute. Add apple juice and cook, stirring, until liquid is absorbed, about 2 minutes.

3. Using a ½ cup ladle, begin adding hot broth to rice, stirring constantly each time, until liquid has been absorbed. Be sure to keep rice at a low simmer while stirring. When half of broth remains, add butternut squash, hazelnuts, basil, and oregano, and continue cooking, adding broth and stirring constantly, until rice and squash is tender and mixture is creamy, about 45 minutes from beginning to end.

4. Remove from heat, stir in Parmesan and season with salt and pepper. Serve immediately topped with feta.

Information

Makes 4 servings

Each serving has 465 calories

For Vegan: substitute dairy-free margarine for butter, vegan parmesan style grated cheese for Parmesan, and crumbled soy cheese for feta

60...Southern Smokehouse Hoppin' John

Black-eyed peas and collards combine in this classic Southern dish that's loaded with protein, fiber and plenty of flavor.

Ingredients

- 1 tbsp. vegetable oil
- 1 medium onion, chopped
- 2 garlic cloves, chopped
- 1 package (16 oz.) pre-washed and cut collard greens, kale or other greens
- ½ cup low-sodium vegetable broth
- 1 tsp. liquid smoke
- 2 cups cooked black-eyed peas, canned or frozen
- Salt and pepper to taste
- 2 cups cooked brown or white rice to serve

Directions

1. Heat the oil in a large, heavy pot over medium-high heat, add onion, and cook, stirring often, until softened, about 3 minutes. Stir in garlic and cook a further minute.

2. Add collards, broth, and liquid smoke, stir well, and cook, covered, over low heat until greens are tender, about 20 minutes.

3. Stir in beans, season with salt and pepper, and cook uncovered for 5 minutes. Serve immediately with the rice.

INFORMATION

Makes 4 servings
Each serving has 405 calories

61...DIY Refried Beans and Rice

You'll never reach for that can again after tasting the delicious difference when you make it your own way with a side of rice.

Ingredients

- 1 tbsp. vegetable oil
- 1 small onion, minced
- 1 jalapeno pepper, seeded and minced (or more to taste)
- 2 cans (15-ounce) pinto beans, drained and rinsed
- 1 tsp fresh lime juice
- ¼ cup water
- ½ tsp. ground cumin
- Salt and pepper to taste
- 1 ½ cups cooked long grain white or brown rice
- ¼ cup reduced fat shredded cheddar cheese to serve

Directions

1. Heat the oil in a medium nonstick skillet over medium-high heat. Add onion and jalapeno, and cook, stirring often, until softened, about 4 minutes. Reduce heat to prevent browning.

2. Add pinto beans, lime juice, water, and cumin, stir well to combine, and cook over medium heat until beans are heated through, about 3 minutes.

3. Remove from heat and, using a potato masher or back of a fork, coarsely mash bean mixture until smooth, yet still a bit lumpy. Return to the heat, season with salt and pepper, and cook, stirring constantly, until piping hot. Serve immediately with the rice and a sprinkling of shredded cheese.

Information

Makes 4 servings
Each serving has 320 calories

62... Cornmeal Chili Bean Casserole

Spicy vegetarian chili is topped with a cover of sweet cornbread in this one dish meal full of flavor and packed with protein.

Ingredients

- 1 tbsp. vegetable oil
- 1 medium onion, chopped
- 1 medium green bell pepper, cored, seeded, and diced
- Salt and pepper to taste
- 1 tbsp. chili powder
- 1 tsp. ground cumin
- 1 tsp. paprika
- ¼ tsp. cayenne pepper
- 1 cup water
- 1 cup canned diced tomatoes, undrained
- 2 cups canned pinto or kidney beans, drained and rinsed
- ¾ cup low fat milk
- 1 tsp. cider vinegar
- 1 cup flour
- 2/3 cup stone-ground yellow cornmeal
- 1 tbsp. sugar
- 1 ½ tsp. baking powder
- ½ tsp. salt
- 1 large egg, beaten

Rice, grains and beans

Directions

1. Heat the oil in a large nonstick skillet over medium-high heat. Add the onion and bell pepper, season with salt and pepper, and cook, stirring often, until softened, about 4 minutes.

2. Stir in the chili powder, cumin, paprika, and cayenne pepper and cook a further minute. Add the water and tomatoes with their juices and bring to a boil.

3. Stir in the beans, reduce the heat to a simmer, and cook until thick and piping hot, 10 to 12 minutes. Transfer to a 1-quart casserole.

4. Preheat the oven to 350 °F.

5. In a small bowl stir together the milk and vinegar and set aside for 5 minutes. Meanwhile in a medium mixing bowl whisk together the flour, cornmeal, baking powder and salt.

6. Add the beaten egg to the soymilk mixture and combine with the flour mixture, stirring just to blend. Drop spoonfuls of the mixture on top of the chili beans without spreading out.

7. Bake until the casserole is bubbly and the cornmeal topping is puffed and lightly browned. Allow to rest for 5 minutes before serving.

Information

Makes 4 servings
Each serving has 485 calories

63... Middle Eastern Falafel Patties

Spiced up chickpeas full of protein and exotic flavor form the basis of this tasty vegetarian entrée.

Ingredients

- 2 (15-oz) cans chickpeas, drained and rinsed
- 1 small onion, finely chopped
- ¼ cup finely chopped fresh parsley leaves
- 1 large egg white
- 1 tbsp. lemon juice
- ¾ tsp. baking soda
- ½ tsp. salt
- ½ tsp. ground cumin
- ¼ tsp. ground coriander
- Dash cayenne pepper
- 1 cup all-purpose flour
- 2 tbsp. olive oil for frying
- Plain nonfat Greek yogurt to serve

Rice, grains and beans

DIRECTIONS

1. In the bowl of a food processor fitted with a steel blade combine all but ½ cup of the chickpeas, and all of the onion, parsley, egg white, lemon juice, baking soda, salt, cumin, coriander and cayenne pepper.

2. Puree about 1 minute until smooth. Add the remaining chickpeas and pulse a few times so there are small pieces of chickpea visible.

3. Form the mixture into 16 patties and place on a baking sheet lined with parchment. Refrigerate for 25 minutes.

4. Place the flour in a shallow bowl. Heat the oil in a large nonstick skillet over medium-high heat and coat the pan.

5. When the oil is hot dip the patties in the flour on both sides, lightly patting away any excess flour, and fry in batches in the skillet for 3 or 4 minutes per side until golden brown, adding just a drizzle of oil if necessary to prevent sticking.

6. Transfer fried patties to a paper towel to drain. Serve hot with the yogurt.

INFORMATION

Makes 4 servings
Each serving has 398 calories

64...Brown Rice Tabbouleh

Terrific hot or cold, this variation on a bulgur wheat dish fragrant with fresh mint and finished with the tang of yogurt is great with grilled tempeh or tofu.

Ingredients

- 1 tbsp. olive oil
- 4 scallions, trimmed and sliced
- ½ green bell pepper, seeded, cored and diced small
- 1 cup brown rice
- 2 ½ cups low-sodium vegetable broth
- ½ cup cooked peas or edamame beans
- Juice of ½ lemon
- ¼ cup finely chopped fresh mint leaves
- ¼ cup finely chopped fresh parsley leaves
- Salt and pepper
- 8 oz. plain nonfat Greek yogurt

Directions

1. Heat olive oil in a medium saucepan over medium heat. Add the scallions and bell pepper and cook, stirring occasionally, for 3 minutes until slightly softened.

2. Add the brown rice and stir well to coat the grains. Add the broth, bring to a boil, reduce the heat to low, cover, and cook for 40 to 45 minutes until the rice is tender, adding a bit of water if necessary.

Rice, grains and beans

3. Remove from the heat, add the peas, and let stand covered for 5 minutes.

4. Add the lemon, mint, and parsley and fluff with a fork to combine. Taste for the addition of salt and pepper, and serve immediately or allow to cool and serve topped with dollops of yogurt.

INFORMATION

Makes 4 servings
Each serving has 315 calories

65...Quinoa with Cashews

The naturally nutty flavor of this unusual grain teams up with delicious cashews and a hint of cilantro for a tasty high protein dish.

Ingredients

- 1 cup dry quinoa
- 1 tbsp. olive oil
- 1 medium celery stalk, trimmed and diced small
- ½ red bell pepper, seeded, cored and diced small
- Salt and pepper
- 1/3 cup raw cashews
- 1 bay leaf
- ½ tsp. ground coriander
- ½ tsp. ground cumin
- ¼ tsp. ground ginger
- ¼ tsp. turmeric
- 1 ¾ cup low-sodium vegetable broth or water
- 2 tbsp. finely chopped fresh cilantro leaves

Directions

1. Soak the quinoa in cold water for 5 minutes. Rinse and set aside to drain.

2. In a medium saucepan heat the olive oil over medium heat, add the celery and red bell pepper, season with salt and pepper, and cook, stirring occasionally, for 5 minutes, until softened.

3. Stir in the cashews, bay leaf, coriander, cumin, ginger, and turmeric and continue cooking for 2 minutes.

4. Add the quinoa and cook, stirring frequently, for 2 minutes until dry. Pour in the water and bring to a boil.

5. Reduce the heat to low, cover, and cook for about 15 minutes, until the water is absorbed and the grains are tender.

6. Remove from the heat, add the cilantro and fluff with a fork. Serve immediately.

Information

Makes 4 servings
Each serving has 285 calories

WAYS WITH EGGS

66...French Herb Omelet

Fragrant herbs and just a touch of cheese highlight this soft and moist omelet that's as easy to make as it is delicious.

Ingredients

- 1 tbsp. light butter or dairy-free margarine
- 2 large eggs
- 3 tbsp. low fat milk
- Salt and pepper to taste
- 1 tsp. Herbes de Provence
- 1 tbsp. grated reduced fat Swiss or Emmenthaler cheese

Directions

1. Melt the butter or margarine in a medium non-stick skillet over medium-low heat, swirling to coat the bottom.

2. In a small mixing bowl whisk together the eggs, milk, salt, pepper, and Herbes de Provence. Pour all at once into the skillet and, using a wooden spoon, gently stir for 30 seconds.

3. Cover the skillet, reduce the heat to low, and allow to cook until almost set, about 1 minute.

4. Sprinkle the cheese evenly over the egg surface and continue to cook covered on low for 1 minute more.

5. Remove the lid, and using a large spatula, carefully fold 1/3 of the omelet towards the center. Repeat on the other side.

6. Transfer to a plate, and serve immediately.

INFORMATION

Makes 1 serving
Serving has 265 calories

67...Going Greek Frittata

Fruity olive oil and the wonderful scent of fresh oregano highlight this Greek inspired egg dish that's delicious with a large tossed salad.

Ingredients

- 1 tbsp. extra virgin olive oil
- 1 medium potato, boiled, peeled and sliced
- ¼ tsp. garlic powder
- Salt and pepper to taste
- 1 tbsp. chopped fresh oregano
- 1 plum tomato, diced
- 4 large eggs, beaten
- 2 tbsp. crumbled reduced fat feta cheese

Directions

1. Heat the olive oil in a medium non-stick skillet over medium heat. Place the potato slices in a single layer in the bottom of the skillet, and sprinkle with the garlic powder, salt, and pepper.

2. Cook the potatoes until lightly browned, about 1 minute per side. Sprinkle the oregano and tomato over.

3. Pour in the beaten eggs, cover, and cook until the eggs are set, but still runny on top, about 10 minutes. Check occasionally to be sure the frittata is not browning too quickly on the bottom, and reduce the heat if necessary.

4. Remove the skillet from the heat, sprinkle the feta on top, and place under a preheated broiler for 1 minute to finish cooking the top, moving the skillet around to cook evenly.

5. Loosen the edges of the frittata with a knife, and using a spatula, slide it onto a warm platter. Serve immediately.

INFORMATION

Makes 2 servings
Each serving has 325 calories

68... Tofu and Egg Burrito Wrap

Diced baked tofu adds flavor to a scrambled egg for a tangy Mexican style wrap that's great for a light dinner.

Ingredients

- 1 tsp. olive oil
- ½ cup diced baked tofu
- 1 large egg
- Salt and pepper to taste
- Dash chili powder
- 1 whole wheat burrito-size tortilla, warmed
- 1 tbsp. prepared tomato salsa
- 1 tbsp. sliced black olives
- 1 tbsp. nonfat plain Greek yogurt

Directions

1. Heat the oil in a medium non-stick skillet over medium-high heat and sauté the diced tofu until lightly browned, about 3 minutes.
2. Transfer the tofu to a paper towel to drain.
3. Crack the egg into the skillet and cook, stirring frequently, over medium heat, until scrambled, about 1 minute. Season with salt and pepper and chili powder, and scoop the egg into the center of the tortilla.
4. Place the tofu on top of the egg, add the salsa, , olives, and yogurt, and fold up, burrito-style. Serve immediately.

Information

Makes 1 serving
Serving has 430 calories

69... Quick Microwave Egg and Cheese Sandwich

You'll never go back to traditional poaching again after you taste the result of this delicious and satisfying sandwich that's great with a side salad.

Ingredients

- 1/3 cup water
- 1/8 teaspoon white vinegar
- 1 large egg
- Salt and pepper to taste
- 1 slice reduced fat American cheese
- 1 light English muffin, split and toasted

Directions

1. Combine the water and white vinegar in a glass custard cup. Crack the egg into the water mixture and pierce the yolk gently with a toothpick.

2. Cover loosely with plastic wrap and microwave on high for 1 to 2 minutes for desired doneness. Remove with a slotted spoon and place on one of the muffin halves.

3. Place the cheese on the other muffin half and microwave on high for 10 to 20 seconds until just melted.

4. Top the egg half with the cheese half and serve immediately.

Information

Makes 1 serving
Serving has 260 calories

70...Home on the Range Huevos Rancheros

High in flavor and protein, you'll love this take on a classic Mexican preparation that's both healthy and simple to prepare.

Ingredients

- 1 tbsp. olive oil
- 4 large eggs
- Salt and pepper to taste
- 2 tbsp. reduced fat shredded hot pepper or plain Monterey Jack cheese
- Two 8-inch corn tortillas, warmed
- ¼ cup black beans, warmed
- ½ cup prepared mild or hot salsa
- ½ ripe avocado, peeled and diced
- 2 tsp. finely chopped fresh cilantro

Directions

1. In a large nonstick skillet heat the oil over medium high heat. Reduce heat to medium, and crack eggs into the skillet and season with salt and pepper.

2. Cook until whites are almost firm, 1 to 2 minutes. Sprinkle the cheese over the eggs, cover, and reduce the heat to low. Cook a further minute until cheese has melted and whites are firm. Remove from heat.

3. To assemble, place each tortilla on a serving plate, top with 2 eggs, half the beans, salsa, and avocado, and a sprinkle of chopped cilantro. Serve immediately.

Information

Makes 2 servings
Each serving has 395 calories

71... Vegetarian Eggs Benedict

Ditch the usual ham and hollandaise for healthy artichoke hearts and low fat cheese in this wonderful version of poached eggs on toast.

Ingredients

- 4 fresh cooked, canned or frozen and thawed artichoke bottoms
- 4 thin slices reduced fat cheddar or other cheese
- 4 large eggs
- 1 tbsp. white wine vinegar
- Salt and pepper to taste
- 2 light whole wheat English muffins, split
- 2 tsp. finely chopped fresh parsley

Directions

1. Place artichoke bottoms on a microwavable plate and top each with a slice of cheese. Set aside.
2. Fill a large skillet with 3 inches of water, cover and bring to a boil. Crack each egg into a small bowl or cup.
3. When water has boiled, stir in white wine vinegar and a little salt. Carefully pour eggs into water, turn off heat and cover. Allow to cook until just firm, about 3 minutes. Remove eggs with a slotted spoon and drain on paper towels.

4. Toast the muffin halves and microwave the plate of artichoke bottoms with cheese until just warmed through and cheese has melted, about 30 to 45 seconds.

5. To assemble, place 2 muffin halves on a serving plate, place an artichoke bottom on top, place the egg on top of the cheese and sprinkle the parsley over all. Serve immediately.

INFORMATION

Makes 2 servings
Each serving has 445 calories

72...Super Southwest Omelet

Fully loaded with protein and flavor, this omelet will satisfy the biggest of appetites at dinner time.

Ingredients

- 1 cup canned pinto beans, drained and rinsed
- ¼ cup canned corn kernels, drained
- 4 canned or fresh plum tomatoes, roughly chopped
- ½ green bell pepper, seeded and thinly sliced
- ¼ tsp each chili powder and ground cumin
- Salt and pepper to taste
- 4 large eggs
- 1 tbsp. olive oil
- ¼ cup reduced fat shredded cheddar or Colby cheese
- 2 tbsp. nonfat plain Greek yogurt
- 2 green onions, chopped

Directions

1. In a small saucepan combine beans, corn, tomatoes, green bell pepper, chili powder, cumin, salt and pepper and cook over medium heat, stirring often, for 5 minutes. Set aside.

2. In a medium mixing bowl whisk together eggs and season with salt and pepper. Heat oil and butter in a large nonstick skillet over medium heat and pour in eggs.

3. As eggs begin to set, use a rubber spatula to pull cooked edges to middle and spread uncooked egg to edge. Cover, reduce heat to low and cook until eggs are firm on top, about 1 minute.

4. Spread bean mixture evenly over eggs, top with shredded cheese and continue to cook, covered, on low until cheese has melted, about 1 minute more.

5. Loosen omelet with a spatula around the edges and bottom of the pan and slide onto a heated platter, tipping the pan to fold over. Dollop yogurt and sprinkle onions on top to serve.

INFORMATION

Makes 2 servings
Each serving has 368 calories

73...Baked Asparagus Frittata

Your oven does all the work in this colorful and delicious frittata that can be made with most any type of vegetable.

Ingredients

- 1 tsp. light butter
- 10 large eggs
- ½ cup fat free half and half
- Salt and pepper to taste
- 1 pound asparagus, trimmed, cooked and cut into 1-inch pieces
- 1 ½ cups prepared roasted red and yellow pepper slices, roughly chopped
- 5 green onions, chopped
- ¼ cup grated Parmesan cheese

Directions

1. Preheat the oven to 350 °F. Butter a 13 x 9-inch glass baking dish.

2. In a large mixing bowl whisk together eggs, half and half, salt and pepper. Stir in asparagus, roasted peppers, and green onions.

3. Pour into the baking dish, distribute ingredients evenly with a fork, and bake until lightly golden and firm, about 35 minutes. During the final 10 minutes sprinkle the cheese over the top.

4. Cut into squares and serve.

Ways with eggs

INFORMATION

Makes 6 servings
Each serving has 295 calories

74... Spinach and Mushroom Frittata

This hearty open-faced vegetable omelet will become a light supper favorite, paired with a tomato or tossed green salad.

Ingredients

- 2 tbsp. olive oil
- 2 cups fresh baby spinach
- 1 cup thinly sliced white mushrooms
- Salt and pepper to taste
- 4 large eggs
- ¼ cup grated Pecorino Romano cheese
- 1 tsp. dried thyme
- 2 tsp. chopped fresh parsley

Directions

1. Heat olive oil in a heavy 12-inch skillet over medium-high heat.

2. Add spinach and mushrooms, stir to combine, reduce heat to low and cook, covered, until spinach leaves have wilted, about 3 minutes.

Ways with eggs

3. In a medium bowl whisk together eggs, cheese, thyme and parsley. Season with salt and pepper. Pour egg mixture into skillet, use a spatula to distribute vegetables evenly, and cook, covered, over medium-low heat until bottom is browned and eggs are almost set, 10 to 12 minutes.

4. Place the skillet under a broiler to finish cooking top of frittata, about 2 minutes.

5. Use a metal spatula to loosen sides and bottom slide onto a warm platter. Serve immediately.

Information

Makes 2 servings
Each serving has 365 calories

75...Italian Eggs in Purgatory

Sometimes called Eggs in Hell depending upon the level of heat you select this satisfying dish with added vegetables pairs wonderfully with a simply dressed escarole salad and a small roll for dipping.

Ingredients

- 1 tbsp. olive oil
- 1 small zucchini, diced
- ½ medium red bell pepper, diced
- ½ medium red onion, diced
- Salt and pepper to taste
- 1 garlic clove, minced
- 2 cups light marinara sauce
- ½ cup water
- ¼ tsp. red pepper flakes or more to taste
- 4 large eggs
- 1 tbsp. chopped fresh basil leaves

Directions

1. Heat the oil in a large nonstick skillet. Add the zucchini, bell pepper, and onion, season with salt and pepper, and cook, stirring often, until just softened, about 6 minutes. Add the garlic and cook a further minute.

2. Stir in the marinara sauce, water, and red pepper flakes, bring to a simmer, and cook covered for 5 minutes, stirring occasionally.

3. Make 4 indentations in the sauce and carefully crack the eggs into them. Cover, reduce the heat to low, and cook until the whites are just firm and the yolks are still runny, 3 or 4 minutes.

4. Spoon the eggs into 2 serving bowls and spoon the sauce with vegetables around them. Sprinkle the basil on top and serve.

Information

Makes 2 servings
Each serving has 387 calories

Salads

76... Lightened Up Coleslaw

Healthy yogurt steps in for mayonnaise in this fast and easy side salad that's great with grilled entrees.

Ingredients

- 1 package (16 oz.) shredded coleslaw cabbage
- 2 tbsp. apple cider vinegar
- 1 tsp. granulated sugar
- ½ cup low-fat plain Greek yogurt
- 2 tbsp. low-fat milk
- 1 tbsp. honey
- 1 Red delicious apple, cored and coarsely shredded
- ½ cup golden raisins
- Salt and pepper to taste

Directions

1. In a medium bowl, toss together cabbage, vinegar, and sugar.
2. In a small bowl, whisk together yogurt, milk, and honey. Pour over cabbage mixture and toss well to coat.
3. Stir in apple and raisins, season with salt and pepper, and refrigerate for 30 minutes before serving.

Information

Makes 6 servings
Each serving has 120 calories
For Vegan: substitute soy yogurt and milk for the Greek yogurt and cow's milk

77...Spinach Salad with Blackberries and Goat Cheese

This unusual combination will have you hooked on first bite while providing a good dose of fiber and protein as well.

Ingredients

- 1 tbsp. olive oil
- 2 tbsp. raspberry vinegar
- Salt and pepper to taste
- 4 cups baby spinach, washed and dried
- 1 cup fresh blackberries
- ¼ cup sliced almonds
- ½ cup crumbled goat cheese

Directions

1. In a small bowl whisk together olive oil, vinegar, salt and pepper. Place spinach in a large bowl. Pour dressing over, toss well to coat, and transfer to a large platter or individual plates.

2. Distribute blackberries, almonds, and cheese evenly over spinach and serve immediately.

Information

Makes 2 servings
Each serving has 290 calories

78...Baby Potato Salad with Mint and Peas

Aromatic mint with potatoes and peas depart from the usual mayo-laden salads and is great with grilled vegetables.

Ingredients

- 3 lb. baby red or white-skinned potatoes
- 1 shallot, minced
- 3 tbsp. red wine vinegar
- Salt and pepper to taste
- ¼ cup olive oil
- 1 cup frozen peas, thawed
- ½ cup fresh mint leaves, roughly chopped

Directions

1. Place un-peeled potatoes in a large pot, cover with cold salted water, and bring to a boil. Reduce heat to medium-low, and cook at a simmer until tender, 12 to 15 minutes.

2. Meanwhile, in a small bowl whisk together shallot, vinegar, salt, and pepper. Drain potatoes, halve, and transfer to a medium bowl. While still warm, add vinegar mixture and toss gently to coat.

3. When potatoes are cooled, add olive oil, peas, and mint, tossing gently. Season with salt and pepper and serve at room temperature.

Information

Makes 8 servings
Each serving has 125 calories

Salads

79...Pasta Primavera Salad

Al dente vegetables highlight this terrific pasta salad version suitable for a side dish or main course lunch.

Ingredients

- ½ lb. whole wheat rotini pasta
- 1 cup broccoli florets, cooked to crisp tender
- ½ medium red bell pepper, seeded and thinly sliced
- ½ shredded carrots
- ½ medium red onion cut into thin circles
- 1 cup grape tomatoes, halved
- 3 tbsp. extra virgin olive oil
- 2 tbsp. balsamic vinegar
- 1 tsp. prepared mustard
- 1 small garlic clove, minced
- 1 tbsp. finely chopped fresh basil leaves
- Salt and pepper to taste

Directions

1. Cook pasta according to package directions, drain, and rinse under cold water. Transfer to a large bowl.
2. Add broccoli, bell pepper, carrots, onion and tomatoes.
3. In a small bowl whisk together olive oil, vinegar, mustard, and garlic. Pour over rotini mixture and toss well to coat. Stir in chopped basil, and season with salt and pepper. Serve at room temperature.

Information

Makes 4 servings
Each serving has 310 calories

80...Sesame Peanut Noodle Salad

This lower fat version of a popular spicy Chinese dish, perfect over shredded lettuce for a main course salad, gets an extra protein boost from crunchy peanuts.

Ingredients

- ½ lb. Chinese egg noodles, cooked
- 3 green onions, thinly sliced
- ½ yellow or orange bell pepper, seeded and thinly sliced
- 2/3 cup fresh sugar snap peas, trimmed
- 2/3 cup fresh bean sprouts
- ½ cup reduced fat peanut butter
- ¼ cup reduced sodium soy sauce
- ¼ cup warm water
- 2 tbsp. unseasoned rice vinegar
- 2 tsp. toasted sesame oil
- 1 tbsp. honey or agave nectar
- ¼ tsp dried red pepper flakes, or more to taste
- ½ cup dry roasted peanuts

Directions

1. In a large bowl toss together egg noodles, green onions, bell pepper, snap peas, and bean sprouts.
2. In a small bowl whisk together peanut butter, soy sauce, water, vinegar, sesame oil, honey, and pepper flakes. Pour over noodle mixture and toss well to coat. Sprinkle with peanuts before serving.

Information

Makes 4 servings
Each serving has 410 calories

Salads

81... Turkish Bulgur Wheat Salad

Bulgur cooks in no time at all to absorb the exotic spices and flavors of the Middle East in this main course salad.

Ingredients
- 1 ½ cups dry bulgur wheat
- 2 cups boiling water
- 1 cup cooked lima beans
- 1 cup red seedless grapes, halved
- 3 green onions, chopped
- ½ cup walnut pieces
- Juice of 2 lemons
- 3 tbsp. olive oil
- ¼ tsp each ground coriander, cumin, and paprika
- Salt and pepper to taste
- ¼ cup pomegranate seeds

Directions

1. Place bulgur in a medium bowl, pour boiling water over, stir well, cover, and let stand 15 to 20 minutes until water is absorbed.
2. Add fava beans, grapes, green onions, and walnuts.
3. In a small bowl whisk together lemon juice, olive oil, coriander, cumin, and paprika. Pour over bulgur mixture and toss well to coat. Season with salt and pepper and serve sprinkled with pomegranate seeds.

Information
Makes 6 servings
Each serving has 330 calories

82... Orange Wheat Berry Salad

Longer to cook than bulgur but well worth the wait, healthy wheat berries have a chewy, nutty character that pairs deliciously with citrus and nuts.

Ingredients

- 2 cups wheat berries
- 7 cups water
- 1 tsp. salt
- 1/3 cup orange juice
- 1/3 cup golden raisins
- 1 Kirby cucumber, cut into small dice
- ½ medium red bell pepper, seeded and cut into small dice
- ½ medium green bell pepper, seeded and cut into small dice
- 4 green onions, finely sliced
- ½ cup roughly chopped nuts such as pecans or almonds
- 3 tbsp. red wine vinegar
- 3 tbsp. olive oil
- 1 tbsp. honey
- 1 tsp. grated orange peel
- Salt and pepper to taste

Directions

1. Rinse wheat berries under cold water. Place in a large saucepan, add water and salt, and bring to a boil over high heat. Reduce heat to low, cover, and cook for 1 hour, stirring occasionally, until tender yet chewy. Drain, rinse, and set aside.

2. Meanwhile, combine orange juice and raisins in a small bowl and set aside to soak for 20 minutes. Drain raisins and reserve juice.

3. In a large bowl combine cooked wheat berries, drained raisins, cucumber, red bell pepper, green bell pepper, green onions, and nuts.

4. In a small bowl whisk together reserved orange juice, vinegar, oil, honey, and orange peel. Pour over wheat berry mixture and toss to coat. Season with salt and pepper and refrigerate for 30 minutes before serving.

Information

Makes 8 servings
Each serving has 375 calories

83... Crispy Sweet and Sour Slaw

Refreshingly sweet with a hint of sour, this healthy, fat-free slaw is a great change from creamy versions and is great as a side for any type of entree.

Ingredients
- 1 cup shredded white cabbage
- ½ cup shredded carrots
- ½ cup thinly sliced sweet onion such as Vidalia
- ½ thinly sliced red or green bell pepper
- ½ cup thinly sliced kosher dill pickle
- ½ cup white wine vinegar
- 1/3 cup water
- 1 tbsp. sugar
- Salt and pepper to taste

Directions
1. In a large mixing bowl toss together the cabbage, carrots, onion, bell pepper, and dill pickle.
2. In a small bowl whisk together the vinegar, water, sugar, salt, and pepper. Pour over the slaw mixture and toss well to coat.
3. Refrigerate at least one hour before serving.

Information
Makes 4 servings
Each serving has 75 calories

Salads

84... Carrot, Walnut 'n Raisin Salad

Sweet and crunchy with a hint of honey, this terrific salad gets a dab of creaminess from versatile Greek yogurt.

Ingredients
- ½ cup raisins
- ½ cup apple juice
- One bag (10 oz.) shredded carrots (about 3 cups)
- ½ cup chopped walnuts
- 3 tbsp. walnut oil
- 1 tbsp. honey
- 2 tbsp. low-fat plain Greek yogurt

Directions
1. Combine the raisins and apple juice in a bowl and set aside for 20 minutes.
2. In a medium mixing bowl toss together the carrots and walnuts. In a small mixing bowl combine the walnut oil, honey, and soy yogurt.
3. Strain the raisins, adding the apple juice to the bowl with the oil, and the raisins to the carrots.
4. Whisk the oil mixture to blend and pour over the carrot mixture. Toss well to coat. Season with salt and pepper, and refrigerate for one hour before serving.

Information
Makes 6 servings   Each serving has 198 calories
For Vegan: substitute soy yogurt for Greek yogurt

85...Picnic Macaroni Salad

Cool and creamy with the tasty crunch of celery and bell peppers, this light twist on traditional macaroni salad will have every picnicker clamoring for more.

Ingredients

- ½ box (8 oz.) elbow macaroni, cooked according to package directions, drained, and rinsed under cold water
- ½ small onion, finely chopped
- 1 large celery stalk, chopped
- ½ cup diced green and red bell peppers
- ½ cup light mayonnaise
- ½ cup nonfat plain Greek yogurt
- ¼ cup white wine vinegar
- 1 tbsp. sugar
- 2 tsps. prepared yellow mustard
- Salt and pepper to taste
- ¼ cup low-fat milk
- Dash paprika

Directions

1. Place cooked macaroni in a large mixing bowl. Add the onion, celery, and bell peppers, and toss to combine.

2. In a medium mixing bowl whisk together the mayonnaise, yogurt, vinegar, sugar, mustard, salt, and pepper. Add to the macaroni mixture and stir well. Refrigerate for at least one hour.

Salads

3. Just before serving, stir in the milk and sprinkle the paprika on top.

INFORMATION

Makes 8 servings
Each serving has 222 calories
For Vegan: substitute vegan mayonnaise, soy yogurt and soy milk for the egg and dairy based ingredients

86...Easy Pinto Bean Taco Salad

Bursting with Tex-Mex flavor, this delicious salad is perfect for lunch or a light dinner, highlighted by fresh ingredients with a touch of crunch and salt from tortilla chips.

Ingredients

- 1 small avocado, peeled, seeded, and diced
- 1 medium tomato, cored, seeded, and diced
- ½ cup chopped red onion
- 1 cup shredded iceberg lettuce
- 1 small can sliced black olives
- 1 cup canned pinto beans, drained and rinsed
- 8 baked tortilla chips, broken into pieces
- ¼ cup reduced fat shredded cheddar cheese
- 1 tbsp. chopped green chiles (optional)
- Dash chili powder
- ½ cup light Thousand Island Dressing

Directions

1. In a large serving bowl gently stir together the avocado, tomato, onion, lettuce, olives, beans, tortilla chips, cheese and chiles, if using.

2. Sprinkle with the chili powder and drizzle the dressing evenly over, tossing lightly to coat. Serve immediately.

INFORMATION

Makes 2 servings
Each serving has 425 calories
For Vegan: substitute vegan cheddar-style cheese and egg free/dairy free salad dressing

87...NEW STYLE WALDORF SALAD

This classic salad named for a famous NYC hotel gets a delightful tang from Greek yogurt to bring out the natural flavor and sweetness of apple.

INGREDIENTS

- ½ cup low-fat plain Greek yogurt
- 2 tbsp. low fat milk
- 1 tsp. lemon juice
- 1 tbsp. honey or agave nectar
- Salt and pepper to taste
- Dash ground nutmeg
- 1 large apple, cored and cut into small dice
- 1 large celery stalk, peeled and sliced ¼-inch thick
- 2 tbsp. chopped walnuts

DIRECTIONS

3. In a small bowl whisk together yogurt, milk, lemon juice, honey, salt, pepper and nutmeg.
4. Combine apple, celery, and walnuts in a medium bowl. Pour yogurt mixture over apple mixture and toss well to coat. Cover and refrigerate for 30 minutes and taste for the addition of salt and pepper before serving.

Salads

INFORMATION

Makes 4 servings
Each serving has 72 calories
For Vegan: substitute soy yogurt and soy milk for the Greek yogurt and cow's milk

88... Nutty Cranberry Broccoli Salad

You'll love this wholesome salad with a sweet side and the terrific flavor and crunch of nuts and seeds in this delicious side salad perfect for outdoor eating.

Ingredients

- 3 ½ cups small raw broccoli florets
- ½ medium red onion, cut into small dice
- 2 tbsp. chopped pecans
- 3 tbsp. dried cranberries
- 1 tbsp. sunflower seeds
- 1 tbsp. pumpkin seeds
- ½ cup light mayonnaise
- ¼ cup low-fat plain Greek yogurt
- 1 tbsp. apple cider vinegar
- 2 tbsp. honey or agave nectar
- Salt and pepper to taste

Directions

1. In a large bowl combine broccoli florets, onion, pecans, cranberries, sunflower and pumpkin seeds.

2. In a medium bowl whisk together mayonnaise, yogurt, vinegar, honey, salt and pepper. Pour over broccoli mixture and toss well to coat.

3. Refrigerate for 1 hour and taste for seasoning before serving.

INFORMATION

Makes 6 servings
Each serving has 230 calories
For Vegan: substitute vegan mayonnaise for regular and soy yogurt for the Greek yogurt

89... German Style Potato Salad

This classic potato salad usually served warm, goes vegetarian with the help of a little liquid smoke and smoked paprika to replace the taste of bacon while toasted almond bits mimic the texture.

Ingredients

- 2 lb. red-skinned potatoes, boiled to fork tender
- 1 tbsp. olive oil
- 1 medium onion, chopped
- 1 tbsp. chopped almonds
- 1 tsp. all-purpose flour
- ½ cup water
- 1/3 cup apple cider vinegar
- 3 tbsp. maple syrup
- Dash liquid smoke or more to taste
- ¼ tsp smoked paprika
- Salt and pepper to taste
- 2 tbsp. finely chopped fresh parsley

Directions

1. While potatoes are still warm, remove skin with a paring knife and slice into thick chunks. Set aside.

2. Heat the oil in a large nonstick skillet over medium-high heat, stir in the onion and almonds and cook for 5 minutes or until softened, stirring often. Stir in flour and cook a further minute.

Salads

3. In a small bowl whisk together water, vinegar, and maple syrup, liquid smoke, and smoked paprika. Pour into skillet and cook with the onions for 1 minute. Add potatoes, salt, and pepper, and stir well to combine and heat through.

4. Serve warm sprinkled with chopped parsley.

Information

Makes 4 servings
Each serving has 265 calories

90... Thai Cucumber Salad

This simple preparation will become a favorite cucumber preparation and goes great with any Asian style vegetarian rice dish.

Ingredients:

- ½ cup unseasoned rice vinegar
- ½ cup cold water
- ½ tsp. salt
- 2 tbsp. granulated sugar
- ¼ tsp. red pepper flakes or more to taste
- 1 large English cucumber, thinly sliced
- 2 spring onions, trimmed and minced
- 1 tbsp. chopped fresh basil leaves, preferably Thai basil
- 2 tbsp. chopped peanuts

Directions

1. In a medium bowl whisk together the vinegar, water, salt, sugar, and pepper flakes.
2. Add the sliced cucumber, scallions, and basil and toss well to coat. Refrigerate for 1 hour, occasionally tossing.
3. Serve chilled sprinkled with the peanuts.

Information

Makes 4 servings
Each serving has 100 calories

Vegan desserts

91... Apple Cinnamon Compote

Enjoy this quick stove-top dessert with a scoop of sorbet for a delicious ending to any meal.

Ingredients

- 4 Golden delicious apples, peeled, cored, and sliced thickly
- 1 tbsp. agave nectar
- 2 tbsp. water
- 1 tsp. ground cinnamon
- 2 tbsp. toasted walnuts

Directions

1. Place the apples, agave, water, and cinnamon in a large saucepan and stir well to combine. Cook over medium heat, stirring often, until the apples are just fork tender, about 10 minutes, adding a little water if necessary to prevent sticking.

2. Remove from the stove and stir in the walnuts.

3. Serve warm with vanilla sorbet or light nondairy ice cream.

Information

Makes 4 servings
Each serving has 110 calories

Vegan desserts

92...Summer Peach Sorbet

Forget the dairy and the extra calories in this refreshing summery dessert with a hint of lime.

Ingredients

- 1 ½ cups water
- ½ cup granulated sugar
- 1 lb. fresh ripe peaches, peeled, pitted, and chopped
- 1 tsp. grated lime zest
- 1 tbsp. fresh lime juice
- Pinch of salt

Directions

1. In a large saucepan combine the water and sugar and stir over medium heat until the sugar dissolves. Stir in the peaches and bring to a simmer. Cover and cook for 10 minutes until the peaches are tender.

2. Remove from the heat and stir in the lime zest, juice, and salt. When slightly cooled, puree mixture in a blender and transfer to a large bowl. Cover and refrigerate overnight.

3. Freeze mixture in an ice cream maker according to manufacturer's instructions. Keep frozen in an airtight container.

Information

Makes 8 servings
Each serving has 100 calories

93...Banana Basmati Rice Pudding

Rice milk replaces the dairy in this lower calorie, vegan version of a delicious dessert that you'll be glad to have on hand.

Ingredients

- 1 cup white basmati rice
- 2 cups water
- ½ tsp. salt
- 3 cups rice milk
- 1/3 cup light brown sugar
- 1 tbsp. cornstarch
- 2 large ripe bananas
- 1 tsp. vanilla

Directions

1. Cook rice in the water and salt until tender and all liquid has been absorbed, about 15 minutes.

2. Stir in the rice milk and sugar and bring to a simmer. Cook, stirring often, for about 10 minutes as mixture begins to thicken.

3. Stir cornstarch into a cup with a little cold water until dissolved and add to the rice mixture, stirring constantly until well thickened, about 6 minutes. Remove from the heat.

4. Mash the bananas and stir into the rice with the vanilla. Transfer to a large serving bowl and cover the surface with plastic wrap. Refrigerate for several hours or overnight before serving.

Information

Makes 8 servings
Each serving has 178 calories

94... Avocado Sorbet

Amazingly creamy without a drop of dairy, you'll be surprised how tasty this unusual dessert can be. A splash of tequila is optional and can be replaced with lemon lime soda if desired.

Ingredients

- 1 ½ cups pureed avocado (about 3 medium)
- 1 ¼ cups water
- 1 ¼ cups granulated sugar
- 2 tbsp. lime juice
- ¼ cup tequila

Directions

1. Puree all the ingredients in a food processor and refrigerate for at least 2 hours or overnight.
2. Freeze in an ice cream maker according to manufacturer's directions. Store in an airtight container in the freezer.

Information

Makes 8 servings
Each serving has 205 calories

Vegan desserts

95... GRILLED MANGO WITH COCONUT CREAM

The tropics beckon in this simple dessert that's full of sunny flavor and great for finishing off a grilled dinner or barbecue.

INGREDIENTS

- 1 large mango
- Juice of ½ lime
- ¼ cup coconut cream
- 1 tbsp. confectioners' sugar
- Chopped macadamia nuts

DIRECTIONS

1. Peel the mango and cut the meaty sides off and away from the flat inner pit. Lay the sides down and cut into 1-inch thick strips.
2. Drizzle the lime juice over and grill the mango slices just to mark and slightly warm. Divide between two serving plates.
3. In a small bowl whisk together the coconut cream and sugar until thickened. Dollop over the mango and top with the nuts. Serve immediately.

INFORMATION

Makes 2 servings
Each serving has 190 calories

96...Strawberry Phyllo Pocket

Frozen phyllo sheets are the perfect foil for vegan pastry making and here it encases the sweet fresh strawberries of the season in a delightfully delicious dessert.

Ingredients

- 1 ½ cups sliced fresh strawberries
- 2 tbsp. sugar
- 1 tsp. instant tapioca
- Dash ground cinnamon
- 4 sheets phyllo, thawed
- Vegetable or light olive oil in a mister
- 1 tsp. coarse sanding or raw sugar

Directions

1. Preheat the oven to 375 °F. Lightly mist a rimmed baking sheet with oil.

2. In a medium bowl toss together the strawberries, sugar, tapioca, and cinnamon.

3. Lay one phyllo sheet on a flat work surface and lightly mist with oil. Lay another sheet on top and repeat with all the phyllo.

4. Mound the strawberries in the bottom third of the phyllo sheets and begin to roll away from you. Half way, turn the ends in towards the middle and continue rolling. Carefully transfer to the prepared baking sheet and lightly mist with oil. Sprinkle the sugar over the top.

5. Bake until the pocket is golden, 20 to 30 minutes. Rest briefly before cutting with a serrated knife into two pieces. Serve warm or at room temperature.

INFORMATION

Makes 2 servings
Each serving has 270 calories

97...Simple Watermelon Slushy

Enjoy your watermelon off the rind and in a glass with this refreshing end to a meal that's perfect for outdoor meals.

Ingredients

- 3 cups diced seeded watermelon
- 1 tbsp. orange juice
- 1 tbsp. honey or agave nectar
- 1 cup crushed ice
- ½ cup sweetened almond milk

Directions

1. Place all ingredients in a blender and puree until smooth. Pour into a parfait glass and serve immediately with a straw.

Information

Makes 1 serving
Serving has 90 calories

Vegan desserts

98... Choco-Coconut Ice Cream

Creamy coconut milk replaces the dairy in this smooth and rich vegan alternative to the usual ice cream selections.

Ingredients

- ½ cup unsweetened cocoa powder
- 2 (14 oz.) cans light coconut milk
- ½ tsp. vanilla
- ¾ cup sugar
- 2 tbsp. cornstarch
- Pinch of salt

Directions

1. In a medium bowl whisk together the cocoa and about ½ cup of the coconut milk to form a paste. Stir in the vanilla.
2. In a saucepan combine the remaining coconut milk, sugar, cornstarch and salt and whisk over medium heat until mixture begins to thicken. Switch to a wooden spoon and stir constantly at a simmer for 2 minutes. Immediately pour into the bowl with the cocoa mixture and whisk well to combine.
3. Cool slightly and refrigerate overnight.
4. Freeze in an ice cream maker according to manufacturer's instructions. Keep frozen in an airtight container.

Information

Makes 8 servings
Each serving has 178 calories

99... Vegan Vanilla Soy Pudding

A snap to prepare, you'll be whipping this up on a regular basis, enjoying it dolloped over fresh fruit or just on its own.

Ingredients

- 1/3 cup sugar
- 3 tbsp. cornstarch
- Pinch salt
- 2 cups soy milk
- 1 tsp. vanilla

Directions

1. Combine the sugar, cornstarch, and salt in a medium saucepan and whisk to combine. Gradually whisk in soy milk and bring to a simmer.

2. Cook over medium-low heat, stirring constantly until thickened. Continue bubbling and cooking, stirring often, for 2 more minutes.

3. Remove from the heat and stir in the vanilla. Cool somewhat before pouring into pudding or custard cups. Chill in the refrigerator until cool and firm.

Information

Makes 4 servings
Each serving has 160 calories

100... Vegan Pumpkin Pie Pudding

Without dairy and eggs, this creamy and delicious dessert will bring back memories of autumn and the fall holidays.

Ingredients

- 1 (15 oz.) can pureed pumpkin
- 1 2/3 cup soy or almond milk
- 3 tbsp. cornstarch
- 1 tbsp. agave nectar
- ¼ cup light brown sugar
- ½ tsp. ground cinnamon
- ¼ tsp. salt
- ¼ tsp. nutmeg
- ¼ tsp. ground ginger

Directions

1. Combine all ingredients in a medium saucepan, whisking well to combine.
2. Cook over medium low heat, stirring often, until the mixture is well thickened and bubbly.
3. Allow to cool somewhat before transferring to custard or pudding cups. Chill in the refrigerator for at least 2 hours or overnight before serving.

Information

Makes 6 servings
Each serving has 125 calories

Glossary and Substitutions

Agave syrup
   Use honey or maple syrup instead.

All-purpose Flour
   Plain Flour.

Baking Soda
   Bicarbonate of Soda.

Cilantro
   This is the herb called corianda in the UK and it is best if you can use the fresh herb rather than the dried type.

Confectioners Sugar
   This is called icing sugar in the UK.

Ditalini Pasta
   If you can't get the Ditalini shape (short tubes) then substitute with standard macaroni pasta.

Edamame Beans/Peas
   These should be widely available (possibly called edible soy bean in some shops) but you can also substitute chick peas or any mix of green beans if you can't find them.

Eggplant
   This is called aubergine in the UK.

Elbow Macaroni
   This is a curved macaroni. You can just use normal macaroni or penne pasta if you like.

Hass Avocado
This is the type of avocado typically sold in the UK.

Half and Half (low-fat)
Use light single cream such as Elmlea Single Light Cream.

Kalamata Olives
Any black olives will do as a substitute for these Greek olives.

Kasha
This is another name for buckwheat which should be available in health food ships.

Kirby Cucumber
These are short pickling cucumbers

Monterey Jack Cheese
For this cheese you can substitute Cheddar, Mozzarella or a mixture of the two.

Phyllo Pastry
In the UK, this is called Filo pastry.

Pita Chips
You can also use pita bread, cut into small triangles.

PKG (pkg.)
Abbreviation of Package.

Pumpkin Puree

If you can't find this in stores, you can make your own. See http://bit.ly/3YmRZ3 for a recipe.

Roma Tomatoes

You can use any plum tomato for this.

Romano Cheese

You can substitute a firm cheese such as Parmesan or even a mixture of Parmesan and Cheddar cheese.

Rotini Pasta

This is a spiral/cork screw shaped pasta, but you can substitute penne pasta too.

Scallions

This is another name for Spring Onions or Green Onions.

Tempeh

If you can't find delicious tempeh then you can substitute Tofu in equal amounts.

Ziti Pasta

You can simply substitute penne pasta for this.

Zucchini

This is the name for Cucumber.

Temperature and Weight Conversion Charts

Weights

½ oz 10g
¾ oz 20g
1 oz 25g
1½ oz 40g
2 oz 50g
2½ oz 60g
3 oz 75g
4 oz 110g
4½ oz 125g
5 oz 150g
6 oz 175g
7 oz 200g
8 oz 225g
9 oz 250g
10 oz 275g
12 oz 350g
1 lb 450g
2 lb 900g
3 lb 1350g

Liquid Measures

1 tbsp ..... ½fl. oz 15ml
1/8 cup ... 1fl.oz 30ml
¼ cup .... 2fl.oz 60ml
½ cup .... 4fl.oz 120ml
1 cup ..... 8fl.oz 240ml
1 pint ..... 16fl.oz 480ml

Temperatures

°F	°C	Gas Mark
275°F	140°C	1
300°F	150°C	2
325°F	170°C	3
350°F	180°C	4
375°F	190°C	5
400°F	200°C	6
425°F	210°C	7
450°F	220°C	8
475°F	230°C	9

American Cup Measures

1 cup flour .... 5oz 150g
1 cup caster/ granulated sugar .. 8oz 225g
1 cup brown sugar .... 6oz 175g
1 cup butter/margarine/lard ..... 8oz 225g
1 cup sultanas/raisins .... 7oz 200g
1 cup currants .... 5oz 150g
1 cup ground almonds .... 4oz 110g
1 cup golden syrup .... 12oz 350g
1 cup uncooked rice .... 7oz 200g
1 cup grated cheese .... 4oz 110g
1 stick butter .... 4oz 110g

Easy Alternate Day Fasting
Fast and Feast Your Way to a New You!

by Beth Christian

ISBN-10: 1482055015
ISBN-13: 978-1482055016

Join Beth on her journey to lose weight and gain a new healthy life with this revolutionary new take on dieting. Beth describes "the simple way to health and weight-loss" where you can lose weight without denying yourself life's pleasures, lose fat while retaining lean mass and decrease your risk of obesity-related disorders.

This book outlines an easy to follow plan which will quickly become a habit just like it has for Beth and her husband, along with many thousands of other people.

Finally you can enjoy your food without feeling guilty!

100 Under 500 Calorie Meals

Healthy and Tasty Recipes

by Beth Christian

ISBN-10: 1482005050
ISBN-13: 978-1482005059

Looking for delicious and healthy meals which will fit perfectly into any diet? Look no further than "100 Under 500 Calorie Meals", the ideal complement to "100 Under 200 Calorie Desserts" and "Easy Alternate Day Fasting".

Beth covers starters, sides, poultry, salads, soups, fish, meat and even Christmas and Thanksgiving meals with her simple to follow and delicious recipes. And for all the dessert lovers out there, there are yet more amazing recipes for you too!

Together with Beth, you're on your way to a fitter healthier life!

100 Under 200 Calorie Desserts
Low Calorie Cakes, Sweets & Cookies

by Beth Christian

ISBN-10: 1490961348
ISBN-13: 978-1490961347

Enjoy this collection of easy-to-make, delicious, calorie counted cakes, cookies, scoops and ices, and pies which will satisfy your yen for sweet treats without piling on the pounds. Beth, a self-confessed chocoholic has devised 100 under 200 calorie desserts and made sure that they included snacks for chocolate lovers and low calorie versions of traditional favorites too.

This is the perfect companion to "**100 Under 500 Calorie Meals: Healthy and Tasty Recipes**" and "**Easy Alternate Day Fasting: Fast and Feast Your Way to a New You**", also by Beth Christian.

MadeGlobal Publishing

Books by Beth Christian

- 100 Under 500 Calorie Meals
- Easy Alternate Day Fasting
- 100 Under 200 Calorie Desserts
- 100 Under 500 Calorie Vegetarian Meals

Book by Other Authors

- The Fall of Anne Boleyn - **Claire Ridgway**
- The Anne Boleyn Collection - **Claire Ridgway**
- On This Day in Tudor History - **Claire Ridgway**
- Interviews with Indie Authors - **Claire Ridgway**
- The Merry Wives of Henry VIII - **Ann Nonny**
- Popular - **Gareth Russell**
- The Immaculate Deception - **Gareth Russell**
- Talia's Adventures - **Verity Ridgway**
- Las Aventuras de Talia (Spanish) - **Verity Ridgway**
- A Mountain Road - **Douglas Weddell Thompson**

Please Leave a Review

If you enjoyed this book, please leave a review on Amazon or at the book seller where you purchased it. There is no better way to thank the author and it really does make a huge difference! Thank you in advance.

Visit the Website for the Book

http://www.EasyAlternateDayFasting.com/
You'll find tips, ideas and more things to help you achieve the life you want. Beth looks forward to seeing you there.

PRAISE FOR BOOKS BY BETH CHRISTIAN

100 UNDER 500 CALORIE MEALS

The recipes look delicious and easy ... it is very user friendly and breaks down the calorie count for the recipes.
Sweetea

I'm always looking for good, clean, healthy recipes, and this book has plenty. Not too many ingredients, not too much chopping or mixing, but tasty and nutritious.
M. Thomson

I'm always looking for good, clean, healthy recipes, and this book has plenty. Not too many ingredients, not too much chopping or mixing, but tasty and nutritious.
"Susie's mom"

Quick and easy to make healthy meals.
Sherry Brossett

ON EASY ALTERNATE DAY FASTING

I love a book that just gives you the information you need and nothing more. This great book was to-the-point with no "skimming" material. So much great and easy to understand information.
Jean Barber

This diet makes sense! Easy and no brainer.
S. Williams

Just completed first week following guidelines from "The Easy Alternate day Fasting" & so amazed at results - best diet book I have purchased!
Maria

Printed in Great Britain
by Amazon